In the Stillness
You Will Know

To the Glenmary Sisters

with best wishes,

Barbara

In the Stillness You Will Know

Exploring the Paths of Our Ancient Belonging

Barbara Fiand

A Crossroad Book
The Crossroad Publishing Company
New York

The poem on p. 30 is from *A Deepening Love Affair*. Copyright © 1993 by Jane Marie Thibault. Used by permission of Upper Room Books.

The Crossroad Publishing Company
481 Eighth Avenue, New York, NY 10001

Printed in the United States of America

Library of Congress Cataloging-in-Publication Data
Fiand, Barbara.
    In the stillness you will know : exploring the paths of our ancient belonging / Barbara Fiand.
       p. cm.
    Includes bibliographical references.
    ISBN 0-8245-2650-3 (alk. paper)
    1. Spiritual life – Catholic Church.   I. Title.
BX2350.3 .F53 2002
248.4′82 – dc21
                                2002004179

1 2 3 4 5 6 7 8 9 10   06 05 04 03 02

In Loving Memory of Clare Gebhardt,
A Friend for All Seasons

"If I was asked
what the gift had been
I should turn
to look at you."

—David Whyte

Contents

Preface

I am being driven forward
Into an unknown land.
The pass grows steeper,
The air colder and sharper.
A wind from my unknown goal
Stirs the strings
Of expectation.

Still the question:
Shall I ever get there?
There where life resounds,
A clear pure note
In the silence.

—Dag Hammarskjöld, *Markings*

The longing of the heart does not go away. One can bury it for a while and busy oneself with other things — the "important" things of career, family, business, reputation, control, influence. But the ache only deepens, the questions grow more insistent, and the yearning simply increases in intensity. We are meant to be mystics, and our souls cannot starve forever. Ours is a sacred destiny —

willed so by the Holy One who called us into
being and who, in order to help us "become who
we are," allows for a longing that will not be
stilled.

We live in an age of great soul hunger. On the
one hand declarations of "God-talk" abound; on
the other hand God seems little thought about
or sought after. Both phenomena strangely co-
exist side by side today — in the same culture,
sometimes even in the same person, who may
not even be aware of the inner dissonance. Both
indicate lack of depth and consequent frustra-
tion. The "same old, same old" is hailed by tired
religions as sacrosanct, often in the name of tradition, when they have little left that stirs the
embers. The "new" and its followers see this as
insufficient and unsatisfying but have little as yet
to fill the void.

Our time is one of extraordinary transition
and upheaval the likes of which have perhaps
never been seen before. The security of age-old
and long trusted worldviews and of the religions
built within their perspectives is literally imploding before our very eyes. Old answers are simply
no longer adequate for age-old questions; new
questions are emerging every day and clamoring
for answers that do not seem to be there or, at
least, not there yet. Some cannot handle the stress
of this uncertainty, and so they talk as if noth-

ing is changing. Sometimes they talk of change but stymie it by their choices — out of fear or confusion. Sometimes they simply withdraw to indifference and hope all will soon go away or at least not disturb their securities.

Much has already been written about paradigm shifts and the postmodern, postmechanistic worldview that is emerging to replace what went before. It is clear that, as threatening as the crisis of our time may appear, there is, nevertheless, also the opportunity for great hope. As I see it, we live in a moment of unparalleled convergence when the great questions of science into the nature of reality and the religious questions into the nature of God are opening up to each other and inviting a common quest. At the moment it appears as if science is the initiator here. Perhaps it has to be so, since it is the scientific worldview that has been the foundation of much of Western thought, including Western religious thought, from Aristotle to now, and it is this view that is imploding. The crisis of science, therefore, seems to have preceded that of religion as such by decades, and we are only now starting to feel the aftershock as the quantum questions of science are beginning to shift the ground for religion as well.

The chapters of this book address themselves to the "aftershock" as it may be felt in the life of believers and as it is being experienced by those who are searching for depth. Thoughtful living today demands probing the interface of religion and science. This does not need to be an unpleasant or a complicated task, though some of the concepts are certainly new and strikingly different and can, therefore, appear strange. It does require daring, however, as well as a peaceful heart. "The light is still," T. S. Eliot observes, "at the still point of the turning world" (*Four Quartets*). The change we are facing cannot be avoided or denied anymore without compromising our personal integrity and the relevance of our religious tradition. When faced with serenity and trust, however, it opens up extraordinary possibilities for new life and creativity.

I stress the necessity of stillness for depth questing and knowing, since fear and anxiety are counter-productive. The new should not be viewed as a threat but rather as an opportunity for experience — one that, once again, invites wonder into our lives and the search for wider horizons; one also that returns us surprisingly often to deep-felt, ancient intuitions for which it now gives us new foundations.

My hope in writing this book has been to help acquaint the reader with the interface of religion and science. This cannot validly be done, however, on the purely intellectual and conceptual level. We first need to touch the deepest aspects of the human faith experience. We need to allow ourselves to connect, quite simply, with our hunger for love and for authentic relationship. We need to understand deeply, through our very bloodstream, as it were, our interconnectedness with all of creation, with the entire universe, in fact, and come to grips with our mutual responsibility. We need also to face our own personal as well as collective sin and our longing to be healed. We need to find there our inherent yearning for the Holy, our experience of brokenness and vulnerability. We need to accept our encounter with loss and the grieving that follows, the ongoing dying and rising that is our life. We cannot do theology authentically without personal experience, nor can we see the relevance of science in our search for ultimate answers without personal experience.

Karl Rahner had it right when he pointed out that Catholicism has been wanting here. It has lacked the art of midwifery in helping us come in touch with those deeper experiences that precede all theological concepts and language. Our "concepts are in fact merely pointers," he says, "to that primal relationship to God . . . at the very roots of existence."[1] Rahner cites many of the experiences I just mentioned and invites us simply to dwell in them — silently, without seeking or giving any explanation. In this way, he believes, we will at least allow for the *possibility* of depth encounter.

This book hopes to be of help here. It was written during my own very personal experience of pain: the dying of my dearest friend, Clare Gebhardt, and the agonizing sense of loss in the months following her death. The chapters of this book emerged out of the questions and depth living that grieving invites, out of the fundamental reexamination that happens when sorrow confronts life and asks "Why?" This book is a tribute to Clare, to the wisdom and love she so generously shared with me while together we struggled for meaning, for reasons, for God symbols during our twenty-year sojourn as soul-mates and sister religious. It was written in gratitude for her life and for her vision.

As many of us know, grieving is one of the most excruciating sufferings we can experience. I have found, however, that grieving also can be a time of grace, since it provides us the opportunity to gather the strands of our life and of our loving and to focus on what really is at the heart of our being here on earth. It helps us to see what truly matters and to let go of what does not. Having been asked to let go of so much in the death of those we love, we find it easier, perhaps, to shed the peripheral. Not that this is done deliberately as on a time-line. It is not really willed at all, but rather seems to befall us. It happens upon us, if you will, as death focuses us on the essence of life and presents in stark relief what no longer matters.

The chapters in this book are about this kind of letting go. They were born, if you will, in the heart of my own experience where they sought an echo in human sisterhood and brotherhood and then reached out to look for wider application and connectedness, for the convergence I mentioned earlier, for the cosmic bond with creation as a whole. They were written separately, with only very few cross-references, and do not have to be approached sequentially. They are connected only loosely, therefore, largely because they all require us to see with different eyes. All, in their own way, point to the common God-quest that seems to pervade all of creation and, because of that, may actually be the reason for the convergence of science and spirituality in our time.

This book was not intended for a simple "read." Instead I hope that it be slowly meditated, that it be allowed to sink into the soul, live there gently, and eventually make a home there. The aim is transformation of consciousness and the deep appropriation of the freedom that comes with vision. As I mentioned already, letting go is never

easy. It is especially difficult when perspectives that
we have taken for granted are being challenged.
Each chapter invites us to some letting go. It tries
to enter into the experience in question and then
to move us toward a new way of interpreting it.
In doing so, it provides either personal experience
or scientific data, or both, to help with the needed
change in perspective.

Chapter 1 addresses sacramentality: the "presencing" of God in human love, care, and suffering; the sacredness of human trust and fidelity;
the holiness that is life lived to the fullest. Without belittling their importance, it moves deeper
than and beyond our institutional symbols into
the existential reality that is sacrament and explores our role as "children of light." Chapter 2
addresses the Christian call to unconditional love
and sees it rooted in the integrity of Christ's encounter with indifference and hate for the sake
of transformation. Scientific parallels are drawn
to identify love as the primary cosmic energy, as
the creator-redeemer energy of God's Spirit. We
explore our fundamental, pro-active role in transformation and redemption. This chapter as well
as all the other chapters stresses the importance of
recognizing our interconnectedness: *none of us is
redeemed until all of us are.* Chapters 2 and 5 support each other. The focus in chapter 5 is on what
is meant by "a eucharistic attitude." We medi-

tate on the essential link between the breaking of the bread and the foot-washing during Christ's last Passover meal and move into the implications of the radical servanthood and forgiveness demanded of us as Christians. Chapter 3 meditates on what I have come to call "the ministry of being." It attempts to move the emphasis from task to transformative energy and explores the extraordinary evidence from science to support the claim that thought is "transmission of energy" and can be both destructive and redemptive even before any action is taken. We can change society; we can change the world, simply by accepting and furthering change within ourselves. Chapter 4 focuses on the ineffability of God and on our feeble attempts at bringing the Mystery to word. With the mystic "we pray God to rid us of God," and then ask ourselves how an approach to God is possible at all. We are asked to allow ourselves to stand humbly in the tension of knowing and "unknowing" and to refrain from absolutizing any and all human images of God. We explore the implications of this in a religion built on finality and dogma. Chapter 6 meditates on the reality of pain in our lives, on what it means to "embrace pain" and what the "consolation" promised in scripture might look like. Does God suffer? we ask. What really is the meaning of "sacrificial love"?

Each chapter intends to open up questions pointing beyond the status quo. I do not believe that answering questions is the reason for writing. Writing invites the reader into dialogue with the questions and issues, to live in the questions presented. Thus it hopes to open up new possibilities. The meditation suggestions at the end of each chapter are placed there to invite this dialogue and help deepen the thinking around the concerns voiced. In a world where "there is nothing permanent except change," nothing is ever finished. That is the exhilaration as well as the agony of our exploration into God.

Aside from my continued gratitude to the staff at Crossroad Publishing Company for their interest and support and to Sandy Lopez Isnardy for the excellent art work, there are, once again, many to whom I owe much. The one to whom I am most grateful no longer walks this earth. Clare's presence, however, was felt very deeply in the writing of these pages. Special thanks to Pietra Hagenberger and also to Joan Marie Sasse for their compassion and care, but also for so generously sharing critical observations and depth insights with me.

To all the friends who supported my candid approach to the topic of grieving and stood with me, a heartfelt thank you, especially to Kay Brogle, Theresia Quigley (Fiand), Phyllis Carlino, Cathe-

rine Griffiths, Anne Warren, and Jeanette Nelson
(Gebhardt); also to Maureen Sauer, Fran Repka,
Diane Reed, Carol de Fiore, Kristin Corcoran,
and to many, many more.

They say that

> ... life is eternal
> And love is immortal
> And death is only an horizon
> And an horizon
> Is nothing
> Save the limit of our sight.
>
> — Author unknown

I

Do This in Memory of Me

One dark night
Fired by love's urgent longings
— Ah, the sheer grace! —
She went out unseen,
Her house being now all stilled.

— John of the Cross (adapted)

Clare's Passing

She is gone now. Yesterday it was a month since my friend gave up her body and was released into the universe. At twelve o'clock three of us found ourselves worshiping together at her parish church. Somehow we could not bear being apart on this first anniversary of her death. We had been together at the time her spirit gently relinquished her body. We had washed it and tenderly wrapped it in a soft sheet to await burial. Now we were, and we felt, like "the remnant." We found strength, therefore, in our togetherness and consolation in our shared loneliness.

I wondered, as I stood there in prayer and recalled her dying, whether the togetherness that
the disciples craved after the death and even after
the ascension of Jesus might not have been similar: *community drawn together out of a shared
loneliness.* Perhaps that is why he left them. Perhaps it was his way of having them encounter
and embrace the Spirit. Perhaps he hoped that
they might find each other more authentically in
the longing of their hearts. Is that, I asked myself,
what church is? Is this where it begins? And does
church end when longing ceases?

As I had worked silently and steadily clearing
out her belongings during the weeks that followed her passing — making room, as it were,
for another to come live where she had died — I
reflected on the extraordinary gift, yet unbeliev-
able pain, her dying had been for me as well
as for all those who had been graced to walk
this last journey with her. Is it possible, I wondered, for someone freely to choose to give up
her spirit, to lay down her life, in other words?
Was it really only Jesus who was capable of giving up his spirit? Some say that this was a mark of
his divinity. It occurred to me that perhaps I had
witnessed his divinity once again a few months
ago when my dearest friend had embraced her
dying and truly, and in so many ways, had directed her own leave-taking with, oh, such gentle

serenity. Was it divinity I had encountered in her dying, or might it be seen, rather, as the fullness of humanity, as the human *ripened into God?*

Five weeks before, the doctor had pronounced her chemotherapy as ineffective. Her cancer had returned, it seemed, with a vengeance and had metastasized into the brain, the bone, the abdomen.

"I will put you on something that will reduce the swelling in the brain and help your speech, but we will discontinue the chemotherapy," he had told her in his usual evasiveness.

"How long do I have?" she had asked, in her usual directness.

He had estimated three months.

She seemed relieved.

Somehow, I now think, she had sensed the disease even when everyone told her that her blood was clear. The scans they finally took proved her right but revealed the illness too late.

We checked into hospice that week to have her medication regulated. "It is time for me to say good-bye," she told me and then gently gave herself over to the task of helping others face her death with serenity. Being with her during those days, I became keenly aware of her hunger for deep stillness. I also saw the way she welcomed those who came to see her — the radiance of her smile, her genuine gratitude for their visit, the humor in the conversations. Some came with great anxiety; after all it is difficult to look death in the face. All left with joy and inner peace.

When we came back home, I moved upstairs to be closer to her, especially during the night. She had grown unsteady in her walk and had difficulty getting up. I slept lightly and heard her every move. One morning she was radiant. "I have come back for you," she told me, "for I have a message to give to you: there is no line, my friend, there is no divide between here and there. We do not die, really; we simply live on in another way. It is all so beautiful. God is so very good."

Beacons of Light

Is it, I have wondered since, still filled with the awe her message inspired, that the "light which we are" simply moves on at the time of our physical death — moves out of our body, as it were, into the universe? Studies have verified that "dying organisms emit intense amounts of . . . light." Janusz Slawinski calls this emission a "light shout" and tells us that it is "more than a thousand times greater than [in a person's] usual resting [i.e., ordinary living] state." This light, he says, is something some persons can actually see. It is not a hallucination: "On rare occasions . . . people have reported seeing this light radiating from a dying person." They saw it in spite of the fact that they did not know the person was dying.[1]

Could it be that our bodies are simply light's radiation locus throughout the years of our life and that, because of that, we truly are "children of Light"? Do we move beyond or out of ourselves when we die, staying, nevertheless, connected to everything? In many respects, so science tells us today, human consciousness seems to have all the properties of light. "Like light, consciousness has no place and no shape. It is invisible, yet illuminates everything. It is unimpeded by time or space."[2] Are the "inner light of the spirit" and the "outer light" that radiates through the stars one and the same, then? Is consciousness the "light" gift that we bring to our sojourn here on earth: "to know like a lover, so that one becomes one with the cosmos reflecting it . . . back to itself," so that ultimately it comes to know itself more fully?[3] Is this what anthropologists and now also spiritual writers are saying when they point out that "we are the universe come to consciousness"?[4] Are we, perhaps, temples of light or, in a more transient sense, beacons of light, of awareness, that are called to illuminate and then to move on (but never away) leaving the world brighter?

If the light rises in the Sky of the heart . . . and,
in the utterly pure inner person attains the
brightness of the sun or of many suns . . . then
our heart is nothing but light, our subtle body
is light, our material covering is light, our
hearing, our sight, our hand, our exterior,
our interior, are nothing but light.[5]

The Silence of Love

She grew quieter as time went on and soon was
confined to her bed since she was no longer able
to walk. Those of us who accompanied her in
her dying visited her room and sat around her
bed often in absolute stillness. "Take my hand,"
she asked one of her friends who had come from
far to spend just a little time with her, "Take my
hand and jump into the silence with me. Close
your eyes and jump feet first." "I did so," her
friend told me later, "and it was as though she
was guiding me into what she was experiencing.
I have never had that kind of experience before in
my life. Honest to God, it was like touching the
very essence of the Holy for a brief moment. It is
awesome to be with a person who is experiencing
heaven and earth at the same time."

At the extremity of prayer words vanish, or
rather the silence-become-word surpasses all

that can be uttered. Prayer becomes the silence of Love, and this silence reveals the "I"
in its deepest aspects.[6]

"Stay here and keep watch with me. Watch
and pray," was the refrain from Taizé that ran
through my mind and deep within my heart as I
sat with her in the night. The Holy Thursday vigil
became a graced reality, and silence grew for all of
us. We began to whisper even when we were not
in her room, for holiness pervaded space and con-
tracted time. It was the pre-Christmas season and
hustling and busyness were everywhere. Looking
out of her window, I felt as if time had ceased for
me. What was going on out there was somehow
of another domain — foreign almost. We were
elsewhere, all of us, keeping watch.

"I will stay till after Christmas," she had told
me. "I don't want you to be alone." And every
day she asked what the date was. On the 25th
her eyes lit up and then filled with tears.

"It is time for me to go," she whispered a few
days later while I was turning her in her bed. "I
love you so." These were her last words to me.
She refused all medication, food, and drink there-
after, and a week later she died. I pondered her
words deeply while I kept vigil with her during
those last few days — consciously focusing on the
love that flowed between us. Michael Himes's ex-

planation of divine presence became profoundly real for me then and sacramentalized my experience with extraordinary energy. "Where two or three are gathered in love," Himes has Christ say, "I *am* what happens between them."[7] The love in the room and, very tangibly, between me and my dying friend somehow in the most literal sense manifested *incarnation* — the creative presence of the Holy One. It is not, I learned during those hours of deep encounter, that when we gather in love, God is pleased to visit us from above. It is rather that when we gather in love, the *love itself* is *divinity present* — *Agape,* coursing in the universe and flowing in and through us in whom the universe and all of creation become conscious.

Coming Full Circle

During her last days her movement into another form of being became ever more intensified, so that we would wonder at times whether she in fact was still there in the room or even in her body. Often we would watch her — eyes closed — nodding and responding to another not visible to us. Her senses too became transformed: beautiful smells, not known to her before, colors that were alive and radiant moved in and out of her experience. She had shared with us earlier that the image of a young girl-child was superimposed on everything she looked at. The child was facing away from her toward the horizon. "When she turns, I will go with her," she observed. And T. S. Eliot's mystical vision came to mind:

> What we call the beginning is often the end
> And to make an end is to make a beginning.
> The end is where we start from.…
>
> We shall not cease from exploration
> And the end of all our exploring
> Will be to arrive where we started
> And know the place for the first time.
> — T. S. Eliot, "Little Gidding"

"We are pilgrims," I once wrote, "Our home is the heart of God."[8] And elsewhere:

> The "dynamic process of becoming ever more fully who we are," as conscious openness in the face of mystery is, indeed, an exploration, a journey into freedom,…a coming forth from the Heart of God and, ultimately, a return to this Heart in what T. S. Eliot would describe as:
>
> > A condition of complete simplicity
> > (Costing not less than everything)
> > — "Little Gidding"[9]

Here, in my dying friend's room, we were witnessing the moment of "arriving at the begin-

ning," the coming "full circle," if you will, when
the girl-child and the wise old woman embrace,
and all, once again, is one.

The deliberation with which she encountered
death was deeply moving for all of us. It was not
forced or willful. It was focused and with extraordinary serenity and gratitude. She was a woman
who had always loved life and enjoyed living.
She encountered dying as a part of that life — a
great, final "yes" to the enterprise of sojourning
on this earth.

> A time will come
> when you will empty out
> into the universe,
> Taking to your heart
> the light of ages
> now and long ago.
>
> You will spread
> as dandelion wings
> into the vast distances
> of past and future,
> And be filled
> with all the splendours
> of the heavens.
>
> You will hear your name
> chanted through the void in
> strange and lovely languages

inviting you to follow
and expand;

And you will be one with them
knowing each, in intimate communion
[as your sister]
as your brother
and your lover
and your friend.

— Jane Marie Thibault[10]

The radiance that pervaded her body even in death, and the smile that lit up her face spoke eloquently of the presence and of the freedom that suffused her being and shepherded her into eternity.

The Meaning of Sacrament

I have wondered, since, where the Christian sacraments fit into an experience such as this. We were taught long ago that a sacrament "effects what it signifies," that it brings about the grace. But what, I wonder, happens when what the sacrament "effects" happens long before it is administered? What if an anointing "graces" all of us who share the holy space and time when "homecoming" happens? What if holy presence pervades our being and our gratitude *is* Eucharist? Where does community begin and end here? Where, in the unity experienced, can God possibly be extraneous? Is it not that God *is* in us and *we* in God? Perhaps this is the *really real,* and nothing needs to be added. *All* simply needs to be celebrated, since *all* is holy.

"This is my body, given for you," I heard over and over again as I took care of my friend's physical needs, as I held and kissed her hands, wiped her brow, and combed her hair. "Do this in memory of me."

"I want burning, *burning,*" God tells Moses in an old Sufi tale where God corrects and admonishes the prophet for his misperception and his consequent ridicule of a shepherd who had wanted to "wash God's feet and clothes, to pick the lice off God's coat, and bring God some milk to drink" in sheer joy and awe before God's presence. The shepherd was, in Moses' view, sadly ignorant of the "proper" manner of addressing a deity, the proper decorum in the presence of the Holy. God suggests to Moses that "those who pay attention to manners of speaking are of one sort. *Lovers who burn are another.*"[11] Could it be that sacraments are truly experienced only in the *burning?* "Where two or three are gathered in love, I *am* what happens between them."

Perhaps ecclesial sacraments primarily symbolize and celebrate what already *is.* This celebration recognizes and acknowledges the reality within the human community. Perhaps they add nothing to it as such because one cannot make holy what already is holy. Michael and Kenneth Himes seem to agree when in their study *Fullness of Faith* they point out that "sacraments are not intrusions into the secular world; they are points at which the depth of the secular is uncovered and revealed as grounded in grace."[12] Perhaps it is more existentially relevant to speak of sacraments as community reminders that point us to the depth moments of our life as such and encourage us to be in them, to live them, to be present to them with authenticity and passion, to experience them to the fullest: our birthing, namely, and our dying, our loving and our reconciliation, our table fellowship and our commitment to witness community in the service of a love that energizes life and makes us one. Sacraments, I am beginning to believe, urge the recognition and acknowledgment of these moments. They do not make them happen. Perhaps it would be more experientially correct to say, not that God comes because we gather in community and break bread, but that we are compelled to gather into community and break bread because God is *there* hungering in us, loving in us, and energizing us in the sharing, empowering us as well as emerging in the loving. God is what happens. God is the *event*. Authentic humanness witnesses

in its very being to the divine and is embraced
by God.

The Emmaus Experience

Not long ago a friend of mine shared with me
the following meditation on the Emmaus story.
It is a reflection that speaks eloquently, I believe,
of the sacramentality we have been considering
here, of the primacy of love to which it points,
of our basic hunger and yearning for authentic
relationality as fundamentally Christifying — in
fact, as *divinity "presencing" itself:*

> They walk together along the road,
> two travelers, silent for a while,
> each lost in thought.
> Neither one knows
> the other's inner life and movements.
> They are strangers to each other.
>
> One begins to speak, softly, timidly,
>   hesitantly.
> The other listens intently.
> The words touch him at an unusual depth,
> intimately, pointing to an ancient belonging,
> like magic that touches a hidden source,
> so that it opens up — challenging and
>   irresistible.

An uncontrollable yearning takes hold of
    him:
to open up, to be recognized,
not to be alone any more.
He finds words.
He dares to speak in spite of his shyness,
because the other follows his words
into their depth.
He experiences the riches of the other
and becomes aware of his own.
Each knows more about the other
than what is spoken.

They speak and are silent together.
Their journey no longer seems long.
They ponder things
of intense and ultimate concern
and lead each other into their own depth.
*"Did not all this have to come to
    pass...?"* —
the paradox of life:
that one loses what one clings to;
that out of meaninglessness
meaning receives its boundaries;
that God's plan for us always first uproots us
only to bring us to a new belonging.
They move their small, individual experience
into the larger interconnectedness with all
    of life.

"Did not our hearts burn within us...?"
Such dialogue does not leave one
    disconnected.
Here the one receives life from the other.

The mystery of relationship:
To be touched in one's being,
with total mindfulness.
To recognize the truth of the other
and allow oneself to be grasped by it.
To accept it with one's whole being
and at the same time to endure
the painful tension created by the sense
that this oneness happens only in rare
    moments.
To say "yes" to the boundaries.
To allow the other his [or her] mystery
until he [or she] gifts you with it.
To be able to wait without getting tired.
To give time its space.
To protect the other
from the passion of the heart
that wants to have everything
at once and forever.
In the intensity of such deep sharing
both feel all of a sudden
that they are no longer walking alone.
Someone is walking with them, between
    them,

glowing with love.
Someone is making
such depth understanding possible.
Someone has gifted them with their
    encounter.
Their dialogue turns to prayer:
"Lord, stay with us..."
Their mutual recognition
opens to the experience of God.
Their gazing at each other
gives way to adoration.
Their journey together becomes a witness.
Their lives, a blessing for others:

EMMAUS

—M. Pietra Hagenberger, S.S.N.D.[13]

The mystics have it that God creates out of Love's need to share. In a sense one might say that "God is not meant to be alone" and in fact creates us in God's image — to be lovers, *that only*. The depth of our encounter in love, then, is divinizing. Our life is there for no other reason.

Death, be it the death of Jesus on Calvary, the passing on of my friend, or of others whom we love has a strange way of focusing us on the essentials of life as love: "Let there be nothing in my life from now on," I prayed while sitting at her bedside, "except love — that clear, undistracted focusing on the other that is care, and kindness, and gratitude; that awareness that brings light into the human family, illumines all in its goodness, and empowers goodness in turn."

"Lord, stay with us," the Emmaus companions prayed as their depth encounter blossomed into Holy Presence, "for this union is fire in our midst. Through it our lives are a blessing not only for ourselves but for others as well. We move into the heart of it all and touch the Divine. Indeed, we live in the Resurrection."

Thoughts and Questions for Meditation

What are your thoughts concerning the following selections from Chapter 1?

1. *"I wondered, as I stood there in prayer and recalled her dying, whether the togetherness that the disciples craved after the death and even after the ascension of Jesus might not have been similar: community drawn together out of a shared loneliness. Perhaps that is why he left them. Perhaps it was his way of having them encounter and embrace the Spirit. Perhaps he hoped that they might find each other more authentically in the longing of their hearts. Is that, I asked*

myself, what church is? Is this where it be-gins? And does church end when longing ceases?

2. *Is it possible, I wondered, for someone freely to choose to give up her spirit, to lay down her life, in other words? Was it really only Jesus who was capable of giving up his spirit? Some say that this was a mark of his divinity. It occurred to me that perhaps I had witnessed his divinity once again a few months ago when my dearest friend had embraced her dying and truly, and in so many ways, had directed her own leave-taking with, oh, such gentle serenity. Was it divinity I had encountered in her dying, or might it be seen, rather, as the fullness of humanity, as the human ripened into God?*

3. *I have a message to give to you: there is no line, my friend, there is no divide between here and there. We do not die, really; we simply live on in another way. It is all so beautiful. God is so very good.*

4. *Could it be that our bodies are simply light's radiation locus throughout the years of our life and that, because of that, we truly are "children of Light"? Do we move beyond or out of ourselves when we die, staying, nevertheless, connected to everything?*

5. *"Like light, consciousness has no place and no shape. It is invisible, yet illuminates everything. It is unimpeded by time or space." Are the "inner light of the spirit" and the "outer light" that radiates through the stars one and the same, then? Is consciousness the "light" gift that we bring to our sojourn here on earth: "to know like a lover, so that one becomes one with the cosmos reflecting it . . . back to itself," so that ultimately it comes to know itself more fully?*

6. *"Where two or three are gathered in love, I am what happens between them." The love in the room and, very tangibly, between me and my dying friend somehow in the most literal sense manifested incarnation — the creative presence of the Holy One. . . . When we gather in love, the love itself is divinity present — Agape, coursing in the universe and flowing in and through us in whom the universe and all of creation become conscious.*

7. *Perhaps ecclesial sacraments primarily symbolize and celebrate what already is. This celebration recognizes and acknowledges the reality within the human community. Perhaps they add nothing to it as such because one cannot make holy what already is holy.*

8. *Perhaps it is more existentially relevant to speak of sacraments as community reminders that point us to the depth moments of our life as such and encourage us to be in them, to live them, to be present to them with authenticity and passion, to experience them to the fullest: our birthing, namely, and our dying, our loving and our reconciliation, our table fellowship and our commitment to witness community in the service of a love that energizes life and makes us one.*

9. *Perhaps it would be more experientially correct to say, not that God comes because we gather in community and break bread, but that we are compelled to gather into community and break bread because God is there hungering in us, loving in us, and energizing us in the sharing; empowering us as well as emerging in the loving. God is what happens. God is the event. Authentic humanness witnesses in its very being to the divine and is embraced by God.*

10. How does the "Emmaus" reflection support the above selections?

II

Love One Another
as I Have Loved You

If I speak with human tongues and angelic
    as well,
but do not have love,
I am a noisy gong, a clanging cymbal.

If I have the gift of prophecy
and, with full knowledge, comprehend all
    mysteries,
if I have faith great enough to move
    mountains,
but have not love,
I am nothing.

Love is patient; love is kind.
Love is not jealous, it does not boast, it is
    not proud.
Love is never rude, it is not self-seeking,
it is not easily angered; neither does it brood
    over injuries.
Love does not delight in evil but rejoices
    with the truth.

> There is no limit to love's forbearance,
> to its trust, its hope, its power to endure.
>
> (1 Cor. 13:1–7)

Undoubtedly, this ode to love from the first letter to the Corinthians is one of the most beautiful passages in the Christian scriptures. Cited at weddings and funerals alike, it speaks eloquently of, and points uncompromisingly to, the hallmark of Christianity: love's primacy, and the insufficiency of everything in its absence.

The God of Jesus Christ desires us to be lovers. We are commanded to love one another. We are asked even to love our enemies, to do good to those who hate us. We are assured that we will be known by our love. We are promised the Spirit whom the world cannot accept but who knows us because we are lovers and will remain with us in love. None of us are strangers to these teachings. They are, above all else, the message of Jesus: witnessed throughout his life and especially on the night before he died — by his acceptance of the totality of his mission and ultimately of his death.

Questions

It is Tuesday of Holy Week, and these are the thoughts that fill my musings. The fatigue of mourning has settled into my bones. Love has a tendency to burn with a raw ache during times of loss, and lately there have come moments when I have grown weary of it all. There is a paucity of words, therefore, that settles into the whole process of mourning and of letting go and hinders the desire to share. One is mute because one can no longer speak. The searing goes deep into the flesh, and there, finally, it finds silence.

What is love that it can ache so much? What power does it have that God wants all of us to surrender to it even unto death and in the face of death — to give ourselves over to it not just in the ecstasy of mutual acceptance, of understanding and friendship, but also, and perhaps especially, in absence, in final loss, and even, as was the case with Jesus, in the face of betrayal, of hate, and of antagonism?

I know of some who, though Christian, resist involvement of this magnitude and intensity. Perhaps they do not know how or are afraid. They fear the pain of passion and practice civility instead. They stop and withdraw before their relationships get deep enough to hurt. They want to "play it cool" and stay in control. Sometimes they may even claim that they cannot get involved because they love "in the name of Jesus." But this, precisely, seems to be what keeps them from allowing their hearts to bleed. I have wondered on occasion whether they allow Jesus to "bleed" for them, whether they "offer things up," but withhold *their* part in the flow of life for fear of losing their freedom, for fear of suffering. They do not allow themselves to enter deep into the longing of their own hearts, or to touch the hearts of others, and so they ultimately wither and die within. Both options, it seems to me — the choice to love and the choice to withhold — bring with them pain. One type of pain, however, allows light to flow through; the other seems a perpetual night.

While I am pondering this, I think of the passage in John's Gospel where Jesus asks Peter whether he loves him. Strange, yet beautiful, this vulnerability between two men! There had been a denial of friendship out of which this question was born. Now the friend needs reassurance. It occurs to me that perhaps *both* need reassurance — Peter, to make up for the betrayal while his heart is still aching with shame; Jesus, to hear the words that make healing and reconciliation possible.

It is clear that one can read all sorts of symbolic significance into John 21:15–18. What fascinates me is that this exchange was even written, and, more so still, that it is followed so poignantly by the call to follow Jesus *even in the manner of his death on the cross* and thus to *glorify God*. I have long ago let go of the notion that a sacrificial death was required for the forgiveness of our sins; that God, somehow, needed atonement — cosmic restitution, as Anselm would have us understand it; that only a God-man could make amends for a sin committed by humans against the divine and thus restore the balance in the universe disturbed by Adam, the head of all creation.

A sister friend of mine facilitating a support group for severely abused women was asked once whether God might be a child abuser. Unthinkable! Yet is this not somehow part of our traditional interpretation of redemption? Can the God of restitution really be a loving God? Is such a God-image even viable today, and if so, how many child abusers justify their actions "in the name of love"? "He whom the Lord loveth, He chastiseth...."

If, however, we can no longer accept such thoughts, how does the notion of "obedience unto death" and of "God's plan" and "God's glory" fit into a theology of redemption? What was it, really, that Jesus accepted in the garden? Where was the will of God in the horror of the cross? Where was God's love? Why was it, furthermore, that Peter was admonished to follow *in love* along the same path and why are *we*, in fact, asked to do so also? What is it that happened and continues to happen here, and what does it tell us about love?

No Greater Love

It seems clear that one can abhor senseless and even punitive death but hold firmly to the belief that there are some things more important than life; some things, in fact, worth dying for. It is conceivable, I suggest, that senseless and also punitive death can receive meaning through this conviction. The four women and six Jesuit martyrs in El Salvador understood this well. They did not die in vain. Oscar Romero too died because there are some things more important than life. For Christians this understanding comes from the Christ-event on Calvary whose justice agenda is ignored when the crucifixion is *merely* seen as restitution for a sin committed by the first human and passed on to the rest of us through conception.

Jesus undoubtedly could have thought of a number of ways to escape the dilemma at Gethsemane. Might he not have been about precisely this as he was struggling with God's will and his own integrity that night? He was a man, after all, who had proclaimed a different path, a deeper vision, who had confronted a system and called for justice, for a new way of relating, a new manner of human togetherness. His teaching had threatened the establishment of his time, and he knew this. People who love power and want it abhor free spirits and joy-filled men and women who live their lives, not out of fear but with integrity and justice, and who choose to give their leaders only the power they deserve. Tyrants will do anything to silence the singing heart, the lover who threatens their violence with integrity and a gentle spirit. Jesus knew "that his hour had come" — the hour when love would encounter hate. Why did he stay, rather than leave the city (in spite of the Passover) and hide with his friends in Bethany?

Is it too much to suggest that the love that compelled Romero as well as the other martyrs of El Salvador to stay and work for liberation, the love, in fact, that has nurtured so many others on behalf of justice throughout history and throughout the world, is the very same love that compelled Jesus to stay and encounter utter hate for the sake of transformation? Were they not all held in its fire because of him and able to surrender to it as he did because of the integrity of their lives bound together in his Body and because of the message burning within them? Is this not what it means to be baptized with the Holy Spirit and with fire?

> For if we genuinely love Him,
> we wake up inside Christ's body
>
> where all our body, all over,
> every most hidden part of it,

is realized in joy as Him,
and He makes us, utterly, real,

and everything that is hurt, everything
that seemed to us dark, harsh, shameful,
maimed, ugly, irreparably
damaged, is in Him transformed

and recognized as whole, as lovely,
and radiant in His light.
— Symeon the New Theologian (949–1022)[1]

"I have come to light a fire on the earth and
how I wish it were blazing already."
(Luke 12:49)

Redemption

But where, one might ask, is "redemption" in all this, where, really, is transformation? What did the martyrdom in El Salvador effect? Has hatred decreased because of the death of Jesus? How can we say that death has lost its sting, that love has triumphed? Are we today, in fact, more loving, more forbearing, less proud and self-seeking because we have been baptized into the Christ? For Christians who truly follow the path he modeled, there is, no doubt, the possibility for a deep inner peace in the face of suffering. What Paul writes about love, therefore, may be witnessed

by them, but has Christianity as a whole been
marked by such love? Are we caught in the fire?
Has the world become a better place because we
believe?

These questions are perhaps too bold and may
be disconcerting. Christianity might be more con-
veniently measured by individual conversions and
good deeds than by global evidence of transformation. It is quite likely less upsetting for
many, and certainly conducive to safe detachment, to proclaim, as does the medieval church
to this day, that redemption was wrought for
us through crucifixion endured by Jesus as the
Son of God,[2] and that faith, though it should
lead to good works, must certainly be understood
as whole-hearted assent to the dogmas of revelation written long ago and presented to us by
the magisterium.[3] Somehow to strive for cultural
and global transformation, to look for results,
clearly visible among us as believers, responsible,
and asked to share in the cross, can be very
discouraging. But what is more real?

> "By this shall all know that you are my
> disciples: your love for one another" (John
> 13:35).

Quantum Pointers to Deepen the Vision

In contemporary times when paradigms are collapsing and almost all models for understanding reality and the world we live in are yielding to radical reexamination, it strikes me that our theological attempts at making sense of the meaning of salvation could benefit greatly from models of perception offered by other disciplines. Worldviews, after all (whether historical, scientific, or theological) have, consciously or not, always been cross-pollinated, even if their religious versions were later sacralized and eternalized in order to slow down decay.

Not long ago, my reflection on the questions raised above brought me, as synchronicity will have it, into conversation with a friend of mine who is fascinated with the cosmic phenomenon of matter's encounter with anti-matter and the observation that such an encounter always effects annihilation followed by radical transformation. We both saw this as the archetypal "death-resurrection" process of creation. The theory of anti-matter suggests that every particle of reality has, in fact, an opposite that is its exact antithesis. When an electron meets a positron (its anti-particle), both of them disappear in an event of mutual destruction and "in their place appear two photons [light particles] which instantly depart the scene at the speed of light. The particle and the anti-particle," says Gary Zukav, "literally disappear in a puff of light."[4]

This mysterious subatomic event is paralleled in the macrocosm in a number of ways. Most spectacular, perhaps, is the phenomenon of black holes,* which, although they are almost entirely invisible, can be detected by the presence of electromagnetic radiation, as well as by the presence of a visible star strangely and mysteriously in motion as if it comprised half of a binary star system. In the latter case, the visible star and the invisible giant black hole actually orbit each other until the latter's gravitational pull completely absorbs the star. It does this at tremendous speed only to release the absorbed material again elsewhere — out of what scientists call a "white

---

* "Astronomers speculated that a black hole may be one of several possible products of stellar evolution. Stars do not burn indefinitely. They evolve through a life cycle which begins with hydrogen gas and sometimes ends with a very dense, burned-out, rotating mass. The exact end product of this process depends upon the size of the star undergoing it. According to one theory, stars which are about three times the size of our sun or larger end up as black holes. The remains of such stars are unimaginably dense. They may be only a few miles in diameter and yet contain the entire mass of a star three times larger than the sun. Such a dense mass produces a gravitational field strong enough to pull everything in its vicinity into it, while at the same time allowing nothing, not even light, to escape from it" (Gary Zukav, *The Dancing Wu Li Masters: An Overview of the New Physics* [New York: Bantam Books, 1980], p. 184).

hole" — but now transformed into a quasi-stellar radio source or "quasar." (Quasars, we are told, are estimated to emit enormous amounts of energy: "Most of them are only several times the diameter of our solar system, yet they emit more energy than an entire galaxy of over 150 billion stars."[5])

The Mysticism of Creation

Reflecting on this cosmic paradox in his book *Quantum Theology*, Diarmuid O'Murchu also points to the death-resurrection archetype: In all of creation from subatomic to macrocosmic reality "Calvary precedes resurrection; darkness gives way to light."[6] Can it be, or is it too daring a thought, that Jesus of Nazareth — for some merely a moment in space and time, although an extraordinary one — opens to consciousness by his "yes" on Calvary the mysticism of all of creation? Could one understand then the love and freedom of his dying as exemplary of a cosmic Love that brings into stark relief the transformative movement of the entire universe? Is this what we are held in — the redemptive event into which each of us is asked to surrender?

Perhaps these thoughts are too bold. Or *are* matter and anti-matter, black holes and quasars, in fact, the cosmic manifestation of creation groaning toward fulfillment? If this is so, the opposites and apparent contradictions of our struggles toward wholeness would, indeed, speak a similar language. Perhaps this is what religions mean when they point to light facing darkness, life confronting death, love encountering hatred and in this encounter effecting transformation. "Bringing the universe to consciousness," perhaps this is what we are called to. In us also goodness can embrace evil (both internally and externally) and, in the embrace — open-eyed, bold, thirsting for truth — compassion is born.

But is there not a danger here of becoming too speculative, too abstract, and of losing our rootedness in reality? I remember sharing these thoughts while they were still gestating in my heart with a group of ministers. One man, visibly disconcerted, wanted to know how Auschwitz could fit into such thoughts. How can goodness encounter the evil of Auschwitz, love the utter hate or "anti-love" present there, and effect transformation? Is transformation even a legitimate concept for this wickedness? Some, I know, consider forgiveness an abomination in the face of such evil. They consider Auschwitz Christianity's greatest failure. Death, cruelty, and hatred of the worst possible kind abounded there. Where were there "quasars" of love? There certainly seemed to be no visible resurrection. In humans, it would appear, the story of the universe can be perverted, denied, and utterly annihilated.

One is humbled by such observations, and the uncompromised darkness presented here seems to leave little hope. And yet! Auschwitz in all its sickening horror — a Calvary a million times over — is not an isolated or distant event. Strange as this may seem and dreadful, *Auschwitz touches all of us even to this day.* It does so across space and time and calls us to conscience — even those of us who did not live during its time of terror, even those of us who were nowhere near its extermination chambers.

The past touches us now, so Louis de Broglie assures us. Nor is there a future that is not already here.[7] The linear, sequential time-frame of a Newtonian universe* to which we have been comfortably accustomed has let us off the hook too easily and for too long. It's linearity helps

---

* "According to Newtonian physics, our three-dimensional reality is separate from, and moves forward in, a one-dimensional time. Not so, says the special theory of relativity. Our reality is *four-dimensional,* and the fourth dimension is time. We live, breathe, and exist in a four-dimensional space-time continuum.…

"If we could view our reality in [the space-time continuum of Einstein's special theory of relativity], we would see that everything that now seems to unfold before us with the passing of time [and also everything we consider as past],…exists *in toto,* painted, as it were, on the fabric of space-time. We would see all, the past, the present, and the future with one glance" (Zukav, *The Dancing Wu Li Masters,* p. 150).

us substitute horror and defeat for responsibility. In the space-time continuum of contemporary
physics, however, all events touch each other, and
nothing can separate us from any moment in
history — not from the love event incarnated in
Jesus of Nazareth, not from the horrors of human
inhumanity. The ancients intuited this and kept
familial hatreds alive with their blood-guilt and
feuds, though the redemptive dimension of this
phenomenon may have escaped them. Relegating
evil to the past absolves us from it: "I was not
there. I am not responsible." Encountering it in
the *now*, however, although it may not bring back
the victims, holds us, nevertheless, connected to
them and helps prevent new ones.

Through the process that Danah Zohar calls
"quantum memory," the past is not a separate
entity divorced from me. It is, in fact, always *with
me*. "It exists not as a 'memory,' a finished and
closed fact that I can recall, but as *a living presence
that partially defines what I am now*."[8] Nor is this
true only for individuals. It applies to nations and
cultures as well, yes, even to the human race as
a whole.

> The wave patterns of the past are taken up
> and woven into now, relived afresh at each
> moment as something that has been but also
> as something that is now being.

Through quantum memory, the past is alive, open, and in dialogue with the present. As in any true dialogue, this means that not only does the past influence the present but also *that the present impinges on the past giving it new life and new meaning, at times transforming it utterly.*[9]

In the emerging quantum perspective of our age, one might say that there is no *me,* only *we* — a we in which the individual identity to which all of us cling with such tenacity is not obliterated but simply shifts focus and orients itself toward the whole. We recognize our unity this way — both in darkness and in light — and, in our at-oneness, move toward repentance.

Studies in holography assure us today that the *whole is contained in each part.* A hologram cut into numerous pieces reveals the entire, original, three-dimensional picture over and over again as each piece is illuminated.* Likewise, we can say that our entire history, both individually and collectively, is held in each moment of our lives (not analogically, but really), and that each of us as part of the human community holds within his or her being *all of humankind.*

---

*See p. 90 for greater detail.

In quantum psychology, there is no isolated person. Individuals do exist, do have an identity, a meaning, and a purpose; but, like particles, each of them is a brief manifestation of a particularity. This particularity is *in nonlocal correlation with all other particularities and to some extent interwoven with them.*

Everything that each of us does affects all the rest of us, directly and physically. I am my brother's [sister's] keeper because my brother [sister] is a part of me, just as my hand is a part of my body.

If I injure my hand, my whole body hurts. If I injure my consciousness — fill it with malicious or selfish or evil thoughts — I injure the whole nonlocally connected "field" of consciousness. Each of us, because of his [or her] integral relationship with others, with Nature, and with the world of values, has the capacity to beautify or to taint the waters of eternity. Each of us therefore carries, as a result of his [or her] quantum nature an awesome moral responsibility. I am responsible for the world because, in the words of the late Krishnamurti, "I am the world."[10]

Moral Consequences

The moral consequences of such a perspective are staggering. There is little room for detachment here — either from the horrors of the past or from evil committed "elsewhere" and by "others." In judging others, we merely condemn ourselves and add to the already existing negativity by our judgment. Revenge, therefore, even public revenge in the name of "punishment," cannot be justified. By it none of us can "put anything behind us," no matter how hard we try, for it only increases the violence of the deed to which all of us are connected across space and time. *The fate of humankind and of all of creation, for that matter, is, for better or for worse, in each of our hearts.* Francis Thompson said it well:

> All things . . . linked are,
> That thou canst not stir a flower
> Without troubling a star.[11]

"The older I get," my friend Clare used to say to me during the last several years before her death, "the more deeply it dawns on me that there is really nothing out there that is not also within me. There is nothing good or evil that I am not also capable of. There is nothing in the human family of which I am not a part — of which I am, therefore, incapable. Not only am I my brothers' and sisters' keeper, I *am* my brother and sister. Their sin is my deed, their suffering and redemption is my story too." The Timothy McVeighs of this world come to mind here, and the Geoffrey Dahmers — both mass-murderers, yet part of the human condition. Poverty comes to mind and pestilence, wars, and famine. As I reflect on Clare's wisdom, it becomes ever clearer to me that our growth into wholeness hinges on this insight, and that redemption cannot happen without it. Through it, quite simply but also painfully, our hearts of stone are turned into hearts of flesh, for we realize that no one is made whole until all are made whole — redemption through all for all. Through it, quite possibly over the agony of a lifetime, we learn compassion.

"Abba, forgive them, for they know not what they do" (Luke 23:34). *This* was the wisdom of Calvary. It compelled the Christ and compels us who are baptized in the fire of his Spirit and draw strength from the one in whom we are held. It is love's star: complete and undefiled, confronted in its utter vulnerability by hatred and indifference to life, ruthless and unyielding, the black hole of destruction. The encounter of sin and its potential for utter devastation with unconditional forgiveness makes transformation possible. This is so at any time, in any age, for the healing of all. And *that* is why God calls us to die, whatever form this death may take for the sake of justice, to suffer the pangs of loss and the pain of loneliness for the sake of love. Ours is not a private or individualistic redemption apart from the rest of creation. Ours is the call to take on the Body, to be strengthened there, and thereby to transform space and time. Ours is the mandate to make up in our flesh what is still wanting in the healing of a cosmos groaning for redemption: Love encountering anti-love for the redemption of the world.

"Perhaps more than anything else," says Danah Zohar, "quantum physics promises to transform our notions of relationship."[12] We are all *one* — members of some larger whole. Interconnectedness is of our essence. What we do to the other, we do to ourselves. In hurting, we are damaged; in healing, we are made whole. Quasars have enormous energy and light — the result of the union of opposites. In us, one might say, this light comes to self-awareness. In us it can be personalized. It can be given meaning and freedom — the power of the resurrection for cosmic Christification.

There are in this attempt to shed light on the mystery of redemption no boundaries, no demarcation points between the sacred and the profane. Creation, all of it without exception, has one purpose and one purpose only: to be drawn back into the Holy One whence it came, there to be divinized as the fulfillment of Love in a movement of infinite grace. Ours is the task, as Pierre Teilhard de Chardin would have us see, of harnessing "for God the energies of love," of acknowledging and accepting its daunting challenge, its complete self-gift. Thus, he claims, it will happen that "for the second time in the history of the world, we shall have discovered fire."[13]

Suffering for the sake of suffering is waste. Suffering for the sake of love's transformative power is divinizing. When life encounters death fully and freely, as it did in Jesus, the end we perceive and mourn, the end that silences us in grief and can almost destroy us, is merely the harbinger, bitter though it may appear to us, of resurrection energy — a form of existence embracing all for the sake of all.

In Jesus, life encountered death (anti-life), and love encountered hate (anti-love). This double embrace brought with it energy of unprecedented proportions, *and we in our brokenness and our healing belong there.* Our redemption and the divinization of the universe are held in this event. Both, as one, are carried by the light and energy of Good Friday and Easter Sunday. We are baptized into the commitment of spreading it further, of carrying it on. Christification is the conscientization of the cosmic unity of opposites. Through it all things are made holy, whole. It encounters hate with love, discouragement with hope, grief with joy, denial with affirmation. It embraces everything negative with the power of being and, through this power, transforms it.

Conclusion and Personal Appropriation

Often thoughts such as these frighten or confuse us. They seem too far beyond the practical day-to-day events of our lives, too esoteric, too remote. What, after all, can *we* practically do about cosmic redemption? How, realistically, *do* we make up in our bodies what is wanting in the suffering of Christ? A story told by Edwina Gateley about her sojourn as a lay missionary in Uganda during the time of Idi Amin may help to concretize our reflection.[14] She found herself, along with a priest missionary, facing a roadblock one day as they were traveling in a remote area of the country visiting the missions. A number of soldiers, heavily armed, ordered them from their vehicle, and rape or even death seemed a very likely prospect. Edwina was taken at gunpoint by the leader of the group into a nearby field. Her fate seemed sealed. Nevertheless, as they were walking, she simply turned to the man and, in an act of complete simplicity and kindness, offered him a cigarette. He was stunned! Somewhere within him, so Edwina explains it (and amazingly — in the light of the barbarism of the situation in which he found himself as leader of Idi Amin's terror squad), the memory of his home and of his tribal rules of hospitality could not be repressed any longer. A simple cigarette offered with kindness challenged the man to return gift for gift. "All he had, however, was his gun," Edwina said, "and so he offered me that." She took the gun from him and allowed him to show her how it worked. Then both smiled at each other and returned to the road. The missionaries were allowed to drive on after handshakes and friendly good-byes.

It is clear that an adventure such as this one is hardly an everyday occurrence. It portrays, nevertheless, what is meant by love encountering anti-love, hate, or indifference and invites us to make our personal applications. Every act we perform, every thought we have, offers redemptive possibilities. We can today no longer afford the luxury of distancing ourselves from depth involvement nor assume the naive individualism that has brought us the callousness and indifference of our times. We know today that we are spirited bodies, relational beings — a unity of presence that no longer permits the detachment of soul from soul, from cosmos, let alone from body. Our thought is energy and affects its surroundings. Contemporary discoveries of inter-cosmic proximity, i.e., nonlocality and, therefore, nontemporality, show us our intimate and instantaneous connection with everything in the universe both now, in the past, and in the future. William Johnston says it well:

> The universe is so unified that every moment or action, however slight, has its repercussions throughout the whole. And [we are] part of this network.... Receiving influence from every corner of the mysterious universe, [we] likewise influence it; and [our] actions are like the proverbial pebble thrown into the pond and causing endless ripples.[15]

The universe we are a part of is an undivided whole where matter and mind are interconnected, where all is one, and nothing can, therefore, happen to me that does not also affect you at any time before and after.

Taking note, therefore, of our reactions to each other, visible or not, becoming aware of our thought-patterns and the positive or negative impact they can have on our environment is of prime importance. Encountering hate with love, rejection with acceptance, bullying with gentle strength is a daily responsibility. The cross we are to take up each day is the intersection point of "matter" and "anti-matter" — symbolically understood, of our inner "star" and the "black hole" with which it struggles in a deeply personal battle for cosmic transformation. We *are*, as Martin Heidegger would say, "shepherds of Being," and our mutual quest for wholeness and holiness implicates all of us. *Nothing* we do can be separated from the love energy that courses through the cosmos seeking to Christify all for the sake of all.

For too long we have allowed redemption to be an event extraneous to us, accomplished for us thousands of years ago and now being parceled out to us in moments of grace emanating from a magisterial church's sacramental treasury. The above reflections have, I hope, moved us away from the circumference-perspective to which such a view is victim and propelled us into the heart of the matter. We are *never* passive in the redemptive event that is our entire life as love, for even our passivity affects us and everything around us. When we allow ourselves to be converted, to be changed, when we grow, when we return love for indifference and even hate, be it at a roadblock in Uganda, in the streets and stores of our cities, or even in our private encounters with friends or strangers, when we allow others to touch our hearts and break down our defenses, when we nurture and care, when we forgive and allow ourselves to be forgiven, when we suffer defeat or illness with equanimity, and, ultimately, when we die with integrity and grace, we touch and help transform not only ourselves or the people we live with, not only the human family or this globe. We touch and help transform, in fact, the farthest recesses of this universe and in turn are touched by it. "Think big!" is what, of late, I have urged my students and the participants of every workshop and retreat I give. Ours is a time when monumental possibilities are opening up for us. They require great vision and big hearts.

> Ah, not to be cut off,
> not through the slightest partition
> shut out from the law of the stars.
> The inner — what is it?
> if not intensified sky,
> hurled through with birds and deep
> with the winds of homecoming
> —Rainer Maria Rilke[16]

Thoughts and Questions for Meditation

What are your thoughts concerning the following selections from chapter 2?

1. *What is love that it can ache so much? What power does it have that God wants all of us to surrender to it even unto death and in the face of death — to give ourselves over to it not just in the ecstasy of mutual ac-*

ceptance, of understanding and friendship,
but also, and perhaps especially, in absence,
in final loss, and even, as was the case with
Jesus, in the face of betrayal, of hate, and of
antagonism?

2. I have long ago let go of the notion that a
sacrificial death was required for the forgiveness of our sins; that God, somehow, needed
atonement — cosmic restitution, as Anselm
would have us understand it; that only a
God-man could make amends for a sin committed by humans against the divine and thus
restore the balance in the universe disturbed
by Adam, the head of all creation.

3. Where was the will of God in the horror of
the cross? Where was God's love? Why was
it, furthermore, that Peter was admonished
to follow in love along the same path and
why are we, in fact, asked to do so also?
What is it that happened and continues to
happen here, and what does it tell us about
love?

4. One can abhor senseless and even punitive
death but hold firmly to the belief that there
are some things more important than life;
some things, in fact, worth dying for. . . . The
four women and six Jesuit martyrs in El Salvador understood this well. They did not

die in vain. Oscar Romero too died because there are some things more important than life. For Christians this understanding comes from the Christ-event on Calvary whose justice agenda is ignored when the crucifixion is merely seen as restitution for a sin committed by the first human and passed on to the rest of us through conception.

5. *But where, one might ask, is "redemption" in all this, where, really, is transformation? What did the martyrdom in El Salvador effect? Has hatred decreased because of the death of Jesus? How can we say that death has lost its sting, that love has triumphed? Are we today, in fact, more loving, more forbearing, less proud and self-seeking because we have been baptized into the Christ? ... Has the world become a better place because we believe?*

6. *Can it be, or is it too daring a thought, that Jesus of Nazareth — for some merely a moment in space and time, although an extraordinary one — opens to consciousness by his "yes" on Calvary the mysticism of all of creation? Could one understand then the love and freedom of his dying as exemplary of a cosmic Love that brings into stark relief the transformative movement of the entire*

universe? Is this what we are held in — the redemptive event into which each of us is asked to surrender?

7. *How can goodness encounter the evil of Auschwitz, love the utter hate or "anti-love" present there, and effect transformation? Is transformation even a legitimate concept for this wickedness?*

8. *And yet! Auschwitz in all its sickening horror — a Calvary a million times over — is not an isolated or distant event. Strange as this may seem and dreadful, Auschwitz touches all of us even to this day. It does so across space and time and calls us to conscience — even those of us who did not live during its time of terror, even those of us who were nowhere near its extermination chambers. . . . In the space-time continuum of contemporary physics all events touch each other, and nothing can separate us from any moment in history.*

9. *In the emerging quantum perspective of our age, one might say that there is no me, only we — a we in which the individual identity to which all of us cling with such tenacity is not obliterated but simply shifts focus and orients itself toward the whole. We recognize our unity this way — both in darkness and in*

light — and, in our at-oneness, move toward repentance.

10. *"The older I get, the more deeply it dawns on me that there is really nothing out there that is not also within me. There is nothing good or evil that I am not also capable of. There is nothing in the human family of which I am not a part — of which I am, therefore, incapable. Not only am I my brothers' and sisters' keeper, I am my brother and sister. Their sin is my deed, their suffering and redemption is my story too."*

11. *We are never passive in the redemptive event that is our entire life as love, for even our passivity affects us and everything around us. When we allow ourselves to be converted, to be changed, when we grow, when we return love for indifference and even hate, we touch and help transform the farthest recesses of this universe and in turn are touched by it.*

III

Let This Mind Be in You

Not long ago a dear friend shared with me this poem by Sigrid Becker:

> I want to have
> You want to have
> He wants to have
> She wants to have
> We want to have
> They want to have
> All want — to have
>
> To have books
> To have friends
> To have money
> To have knowledge
> To have power
> To have recognition
> To have love
>
> HE wanted to be
> to be obedient
> to be faithful
> to be small

to be poor
to be Love
to be forgiveness
to be hope
to be the friend of all

to be *so much*
that finally
he had nothing left
not even himself,
But God had him
and
HE STILL IS.
I also want to be,
So that He will have me.[1]

The reign of God means *being* totally, *being* so much that there is no-thing left to *have*. It means not even having oneself — giving oneself up completely, in utter surrender. It means *being possessed by God.* Our life is for this and for nothing else, and our death — accepted creatively as it was by my friend, in complete one-ness with Him — is indeed the final "yes" to this outpouring, a moment of *ec-stasis,* of standing beyond oneself, completely and finally, into the Light. The reign of God calls us to itself and calls us for no other reason.

On Being and Doing

Becker's poetic comparison between being and having speaks to authenticity: a progressive movement from immaturity and insecurity, from possessiveness and superficiality to a depth that was most poignantly identified in Christ Jesus but draws all of us into inwardness. Unfortunately theological and ecclesial thought rarely touches upon, let alone finds itself at home in, the grace-filled speech of poets. In the apparent interest of clarity, many of us tend to move away from their depth and all too often propose distinctions that obfuscate rather than clarify. Thus we can at times unwittingly betray the experience under consideration rather than bring it to light.

The distinction some of us draw between *being* and *doing* in our reflections on ministry and service seems to me a case in point. The call to ministry, it is said, is about direct action — public, at that[2] — not about *being* as such. We are ever called to a life of service, Thomas F. O'Meara tells us, and because of that merely *being* a good Christian is not enough. "A Christian is not baptized into a tribe or race or into a passive group of neophytes or into a gnostic study club," he points out, "but into an active community: into church but also into service in the church."[3]

Clearly one cannot quarrel with this observation. I wonder, however, whether "merely *being* a Christian" is really that insignificant in the redemptive plan of God and whether it should be that easily dismissed. Perhaps the paradoxical approach of seeing the relationship between being and doing rather than their difference or even their mutual exclusion might be more helpful and empowering. Could it not be that Sigrid Becker with her poetic insight offers us a deeper and often neglected "take" that looks into the essence of this issue by *including* rather than by *excluding* and thus succeeds in preserving a dynamic that can easily escape us?

Why should *being* as such imply passivity? "He wanted to *be*, to be obedient, to be faithful, to be small, to be poor, to be Love, to be forgiveness, to be hope, to be the friend of all, to be so much that finally he had nothing left, not even himself." This kind of *being,* I propose — *His* being — is replete with energy. It is action-filled, released from possessiveness, control, and power. It is transformative, in fact, and speaks, I believe, to the essence of the universe, to the dynamic call of creation.

In an interesting little book entitled *Holiness,* Donald Nicholl affirms this. He sees the whole purpose, not only of the human being, but of all of creation, in fact, as mirrored in and addressed by what Becker in her poem identifies

as *being*. Whatever *is*, Nicholl suggests, moves in
the long chain of evolution toward its own self-
transcendence, emptying itself out, giving itself
up in its very act of being, always toward the
greater fulfillment of creation itself. The inanimate, if you will, gives itself up, yields, opens up
toward life; life toward consciousness, consciousness toward self-awareness, toward light. This
process of "being-as-self-gift" reached its climax,
he tells us, in the fullness of time (and, equally,
the fullness of *being*) when "self-aware life" in
total freedom and love gave itself up through one
man and for the sake of love and thus brought
creation to its deepest truth, the union, I would
add, of light and love.

> In no time the universe came into being; and
> then there was time. Being and time are con-
> comitant. But time has a different quality, a
> different intensity, according to the kind of
> being with which it is concomitant. Starting
> from point Alpha the quality of being, and
> therefore of time, intensifies as inert matter
> is transcended by life, and life by conscious-
> ness, and so forth with intensifying steepness
> until the climax is achieved (Omega) *through
> a self-conscious being who sacrifices him-
> self for the sake of others.* No being, neither
> man [nor woman] nor God can go any fur-

ther; there is no further to go. That is the
end of time. Once more, as in the beginning,
it is no time, because both being and time
have now been totally transcended: they are
fulfilled.[4]

Almost as if by intuition we celebrate this truth
at the Easter Vigil each year when in the light of
the Easter candle we proclaim: "Christ yesterday
and today, the beginning and the end, Alpha and
Omega; all time belongs to him, and all ages, to
him be glory and power through every age and
forever, Amen." Our call, and we may know this
only dimly at times, is to live into the sacred paradox of this moment of fulfillment that is coming
toward us out of our past (the history of our tradition); that is realized and also is not yet; that
has completed and transcended time even as it
holds us in its flow.

If human beings are indeed the embodiment
of a "cosmos come to consciousness," then Jesus
Christ stands for its ultimate fulfillment in love's
conscious self-gift. He speaks the creative Word.
He *is* the fullness of the story that is the universe
unfolding and God's breakthrough into time and
space as Love. Here we hear Paul's insistence that
"from the beginning until now the entire creation has been groaning in one great act of giving
birth" (Rom. 8:22), and we come to know that

being held in this cosmic travail of love is the grace of our heritage in Christ.

Richard P. McBrien points to this heritage when in *Catholicism* he sees "the human community and the entire world in which the human community exists [as] oriented toward Christ and ... sustained by him." He insists that "there is no creation except in view of Christ. There is no human existence, therefore, except in view of Christ and of our New Covenant in Christ."[5] Jesus as the Christ, transhistorically, if you will,[6] embraces in his salvific presence all of creation, from the beginning to now and for all ages to come. In Christ, therefore, is the fullness of creation, the end of evolution, the eschaton. In his outpouring, "He still is," as Becker puts it. Ours is the call to claim the power of this truth and enflesh it in *our* time and space.

Martha Reeves speaks powerfully to this:

We who are created in the image-without-image of the Ineffable need to be aware that our truth is a mirror of God's truth. It can emerge only to the degree to which we allow this same divine self-outpouring to be the movement of our lives. Like God, we must engage in the same act of gaining identity through self-forgetfulness. If we are to be truly who we are, this continual dispossession must become our essential dynamic. To put this truth in another perspective, the ineffability of God, neighbor and self is the *same ineffability*, the same mystery. It is the divine being poured out through us in all its variation and unity.[7]

For Christians this means "putting on the Christ." Our living in the fullness of time means moving toward its realization every day anew. Living into the Christ is bringing about God's reign even as we recognize it already in our midst.

> I want to *be* that way
> to *be* so much
> that finally
> I have nothing left
> not even myself,
>
> But God will have me
> and I will *be* still
>
> I also want to *be,*
> So that He will have me.

Science and the Ministry of Being

Is ministry public service in the church for the sake of God's reign, or can it be found also in the "being" described above? Could our understanding of "ministry," in other words, be expanded

not merely to "service" of all kinds for the betterment of the human condition even if not publicly
recognized and ordered by the church, but even
to mere "being," identified simply by its transformative effects and on the grounds solely of its
transformative power? Could "being," in other
words, be ministerial?

The "field theory" of contemporary science
might help to clarify this. For it to be able to
do this, however, we must first accept the fact
that what Brian Swimme calls our age-old "subtle
and sometimes outright bias against non-human
nature" will need to be suspended.

> The great news of our time is the evolution-
> ary story in which we come to realize that
> we humans are all embedded in a living, de-
> veloping universe, and that we are therefore
> cousins to everything in the universe. To em-
> ploy theological language emphasizing our
> separation from the universe is to burden our
> endeavor with unnecessary baggage.[8]

Field theory speaks to the "being dimension"
of all of reality as relational and points to its
extraordinary power of influence. It proposes invisible forces that organize visible reality — the
visible universe. This is how Rupert Sheldrake
describes the transformative process:

Morphogenetic fields shape and direct the entire animate and inanimate creation. And although the *fields are free of matter and energy, they still have an effect on space and time,* and can even be changed over space and time. If a member of a biological species acquires a new behavior [this usually comes about through what Sheldrake elsewhere calls "a creative jump," and in humans one might call "creative insight" or "inspiration"], its morphogenetic field will be altered. *If it retains its new behavior long enough, the morphic resonance will set up a reciprocal effect among all the members of the whole species.* The morphogenetic fields are the actual cause of the order, regularity, and constancy of the universe — but they can *also admit wholly new modes and forms of behavior.*[9]

When Willigis Jäger meditates on the transformative power of fields, he concludes that if change is effected by fields and not by causes, as we were led to believe within the Newtonian worldview of the modern era, then physiology and biology, in fact materiality as such, must yield to deeper realities.[10] Teilhard de Chardin suggested this years ago: "Concretely speaking there is no matter and spirit; rather there exists only *matter*

that is becoming spirit. The stuff of the universe
is spirit-matter."[11]

The cosmic influence of fields opens us to new
insights regarding depth transformation. Margaret Wheatley sees the *vision,* or what above
I referred to as the "insight," of an individual as well as of a group metaphorically as a
"field" that has transformative power not just
within the group but far beyond it.[12] *Vision* is
a "being dimension" of human interrelationality.
It emerges out of thought and is intimately related to depth awareness. Thought, if you will, is
energy: it is transmission and can, therefore, be
both destructive and redemptive. William Johnston's observation that the "Zen Master sits for
the universe" takes on an entirely new significance within this context. When we reflect and
deepen our awareness and certainly, as Johnston observes, when we sit in prayer, "the very
highest form of human energy is brought into
play, a human energy that is nothing other than
love at the core of one's being. It is precisely
this," he insists, *"that builds the earth....* Here a
whole cosmic energy is unleashed and the whole
world shakes. More things are wrought by prayer
than this world dreams of."[13] Jäger carries this
thought even further by suggesting that "we can
change humanity, society, and the world [simply]
by our sitting and changing ourselves."[14] Prayer,

then, is not merely a way of talking to God, petitioning help, or even praising — something we *do*. Our being in prayer is transformative in itself, and personal transformation — developing an interior life, the expanding of our own consciousness and power to love, sending forth life-giving and empowering good will, in other words, authentic being — *is* cultural as well as cosmic transformation.

It would seem that the discoveries of contemporary science present us with realities that fundamentally challenge dualistic restrictions that, up to now, limited our view of service to the strict realm of public action, preferably with measurable success. If simply *being* can be transformative and helps open the channels for grace, the "ministry of being" can be a very real and viable possibility, and the notion of "call" expands as well. Without doing away with or diminishing their importance, it moves beyond public or ecclesial "commissioning" to apostolic action, works of charity, and concrete witnessing in order to include the depth call to inner work, silent prayer, personal conversion, and the expansion of consciousness for the sake of love and for the divinization of all of creation.

Expanding the Meaning of Community and Call

It would seem to me that the meaning of community also expands in the light of these observations and points far beyond a structured group as such. I am reminded here of the remarks by Jim Wallace, the Indian guide in the film *I Heard the Owl Call My Name,* when he is describing his village to the new vicar. "My village is so big it never gets rained on," he says, "because the rain is my village too, and the wind, and the sea. All the history of my tribe and all its legends is my village too. And me, I am the village, and the village is me."

Authentic community is as wide as the *cosmos groaning for redemption.* "Our awakening," John of the Cross reminds us, "is an awakening of God, and our uprising is an uprising of God," to which Willigis Jäger adds: "The awakening of society is an awakening of God in society. The awakening of the cosmos is an awakening of God in the evolution of the cosmos." Expanding on Karl Rahner, he predicts that "human beings of the future (not just Christians of the future) will be enlightened people." They will, in other words, embrace a responsibility far greater than merely the faithful execution of a designated task, no matter how important it might be. They will accept their fundamental destiny toward personal and, therefore, toward cosmic wholeness. "They will be mystics. That is our sole chance of survival."[15] That is, in fact, our deepest call. It is no rare exception — gift to a select few, but can be responded to by everyone, as each of us in turn, through his or her own way of expanding awareness, of being and doing, contributes toward reaching the "critical mass"* necessary to effect the transformation of all.

The mystical path is the path of *being*, the path of enlightenment, which, in the process of self-emptying, affirms the very purpose of creation itself and thus helps bring it about, returning, as it were, all things to their rightful place. Deep down in the mystic's heart is recognized

> a yearning that is the Divine itself. God presses toward unfolding in us....We seek the roots of our existence because we have forgotten who we really are. That is why we go out and search until we learn that we have already been found. We aren't seekers at all; we're the sought.[16]

---

*The scientific notion of "critical mass" might be understood most easily when one sees it as that dynamic culmination point within a system (a whole) when sufficient momentum has been gathered through the cumulative activity of the parts to effect change in the entire system (in the whole).

Call and the salvific effects of our "yes" expose
us in the most profound sense, I believe, to this
encounter of the seeker and the found deep within
each one of us. We say "yes" to wanting to *be*
like Him: wanting to *be* so *much* that finally we
have nothing left, not even ourselves, and in our
yearning that this be so we find that we have,
in fact, already been found; that He *has* us; that
with Him we *are* still and remain even now. We
have come home and with us, ever more fully, the
whole universe.

"Life itself is a call," my dearest friend told me
as she was wrestling with the ever more debilitating effects of cancer moving her toward death.
"You go through it, and its terrors turn to opportunities for grace. Cancer too is an event that
takes us into God. Life gets thinner, less cluttered,
when one experiences serious illness and suffering. One's priorities change and get fewer. The
veil becomes more transparent. *Being* with whatever *is* will lead us into depths totally unknown."
There is a homecoming here and a reconciliation
that has us reach beyond ourselves and gifts us
with the sacred yet mysterious power of touching the world. And here it is precisely where we
can find an experience of call that far surpasses
all theological distinctions between "mere being"
and ministry or service as publicly designated
"for the church and by the church." "I have ar-

rived," says Thich Nhat Hanh. "I am home, in
the here, in the now. I am solid. I am free. In the
ultimate I dwell,"[17] and, one might add, "the ultimate dwells in me toward the transformation of
everything."

Transcending Past Boundaries

One's boundaries are expanded in this experience
of depth call, and the world, even the universe,
becomes one's home. There is a sense of belonging to the whole; of containing the whole, in fact;
of a deep responsibility, therefore, that involves
the totality that is, has been, and will be.

Within the Newtonian-Cartesian paradigm of
the modern world as we know it, claims of
this kind may seem exaggerated at best. Identity
is achieved through parameters and by exclusion. Our tasks define us. Goals are set and
are achieved. Seeing oneself as part of a larger
whole implies significance or insignificance in direct proportion to one's influence or lack thereof
within the structures and objectives of that whole.
There is for us a cause-and-effect sequence to
much of what we do, even to our prayers and
to the liturgical life of our church. Few of us
would dream that our personal behavior, even
our most hidden thought patterns, our inner
work as such, can bring about change to any-

one outside of ourselves, let alone to the whole of which we see ourselves merely as a tiny and mostly unimportant part.

We belong to a church that, even if it calls itself a body, clearly understands itself according to the norms identified above. It is and it acts as an organization with many distinct parts, all of which have their place of importance and are ordered accordingly. Ministerial action is allowed to some and denied to others according to their place within the organization. Change is effected slowly, deliberately, and through proper channels. Traditions are not only revered but often seen as normative. Variations are regarded with suspicion, and sudden alterations in behavior and outlook, Sheldrake's "creative jumps," are rarely if ever accepted. Most organized religions follow the pattern described here; some more so than others. For many it has been sacralized. Structures are seen as safeguarding, even as producing, order and harmony. They are to be preserved. Such views are strengthened wherever God is seen as unmoved mover and uncaused cause. Permanence becomes holy, then, and change is seen as fickle and untrustworthy.

The dynamic and ever changing flow of reality as organism rather than organization and of God as creative love energy permeating all of creation are concepts that take major adjustment.

Often resistance to them is easier than acceptance. Yet Rahner's and Jäger's reflections come to mind once again: Become a mystic, or perish! Mystics, it seems, have always seen things from a more radical perspective. "Everything that is in the heavens, on the earth, and under the earth," says Hildegard of Bingen, "is penetrated with connectedness, penetrated with relatedness."[18] And William Johnston, writer on both Christian and Zen mystical experience, adds to this his observation that "the universe is so unified that every moment or action, however slight, has its repercussions throughout the whole. And [we are] part of this network. . . . Receiving influence from every corner of the mysterious universe, [we] likewise influence it." He compares our actions to the "proverbial pebble thrown into the pond and causing endless ripples."[19] The responsibility that this view calls for, even as it seems to democratize power for change, is staggering. We are all pulled into the dialectic of growth here. Our very *being* affects reality all around us and is affected by it for better or for worse. *We matter,* and all of creation takes note and counts on us.

Mystical intuition, as is becoming ever clearer in our time, receives strong support in all of this from the postmodern, postmechanistic theories and discoveries of science that, as it were, "happened upon us" quite unexpectedly during the twentieth century, preparing the way for a totally new worldview at the beginning of the new millennium. The "whole is in the part," the world-renowned physicist David Bohm tells us,[20] confronting the commonsense perception that shows the whole as the sum of its parts. Holographic experiments, as I have mentioned already, concretize his observation with surprising clarity. To expand on my earlier observation: A hologram is perhaps most easily understood as a three-dimensional picture obtained via a split laser beam. While the first beam is bounced off the desired object, the other beam is allowed to collide with the reflected light causing what is called an interference pattern. When this is recorded on film and yet another laser beam made to shine through this film, a three-dimensional picture of the original object is the result. What is remarkable and significant in a hologram is the fact that, unlike an ordinary photograph which, if cut into a number of pieces, will yield only partial images of the whole for each piece, the cut-up pieces of holographic film will each yield the entire three-dimensional picture,[21] thus illustrating that, indeed, the whole is contained in each of its parts.

Challenges to Theology

Discoveries such as these "push our horizons" beyond physics into the depth reality of existence and stretch us far beyond our perceptual as well as conceptual frame of reference. A physics that discovers reality as interlaced and interwoven, that discovers the presence of the whole in each part and each part connected to every other part, that sees mind and matter as, in fact, inextricably linked with each part of the universe, containing, in some sense, the entire universe,[22] challenges a metaphysics of exclusion and triumphalism to its very core by the utter and uncompromising relationality that it presents as foundational to all of reality. The implications of this are staggering, for as the science that was normative for so much of our modern worldview literally implodes, the theology built on its dicta needs to reexamine its perspectives as well or become irrelevant and obsolete with it.

What previous theories have presented to us as self-evident and as foundational for any realistic interpretation of our world and of our worldview needs in our time, therefore, to be put to the test once again and must yield to sincere rethinking. The notion of ministry, for example, that puts excessive emphasis on visible action and regards the personal life of the minister, if not as

N. B.
previous
? ex
opera
operato

unimportant, then at most as secondary to the
effects of his or her words and deeds will find
its credibility seriously questioned. If the whole
is in the part, no one with whom I minister or
for whom I pray, no one I think about, in fact,
and not even the person I do not think about is
separate from me, from my interiority, from my
brokenness, and from my redemption, nor is the
cosmos whose transformation I am about, nor is
the God to whom I pray. If interconnectedness —
at-onement, is the fabric of reality as a whole, we
cannot stand apart from one another in any way
or for any reason and still be authentic ourselves.
If *being* is transformative, the call to authenticity can no longer be merely an exhortation to
personal holiness but speaks, in fact, of cosmic
ramifications. Baptism (and its extension especially into Eucharist, Holy Orders, Confirmation,
and Matrimony) becomes within this perspective
a *dynamic event* that takes "being grafted into
the Christ" literally — seeing the Christ event as
the creative outpouring of God to which we, as
"creation come to consciousness," belong in the
most intimate expression of love.

If it is true, as Danah Zohar (describing John
Stewart Bell's nonlocality theory) assures us, that
"all things and all moments touch each other at
every point,"[23] then all of us can say and can experience that we partake truly, beyond space and

time, in the Christ energy incarnate historically in Jesus of Nazareth. It flows through us who are, in fact, nonlocally and nontemporally connected to Him. It permeates our flesh, as well as our spirits — living signs of the God of our longing, sacraments for the healing and wholeness of the world toward the Christification of the universe.

"Become who you *are,*" the wisdom figure exhorts us, therefore, knowing the glory to which we are called and in which we are held already and at each moment of our lives. "Become who you *are,*" reconciling and shepherding within you the forgotten treasure of *being.*

Thoughts and Questions for Meditation

What are your thoughts concerning the following selections from chapter 3?

1. *The reign of God means being so much that there is no-thing left to have. It means not even having oneself — giving oneself up completely, in utter surrender, being possessed by God. Our life is for this and for nothing else.*

2. *Is ministry public service in the church for the sake of God's reign, or can it be found also in "being" as such? Could our understanding of "ministry," in other words, be*

expanded not merely to "service" of all kinds for the betterment of the human condition even if not publicly recognized and ordered by the church, but even to mere "being," identified simply by its transformative effects and on the grounds solely of its transformative power? Could "being," in other words, be ministerial?

3. *The cosmic influence of fields opens us to new insights regarding depth transformation. Margaret Wheatley sees the vision or insight of an individual as well as of a group metaphorically as a "field" that has transformative power not just within the group but far beyond it. Vision is a "being dimension" of human interrelationality.... When we reflect and deepen our awareness and certainly, as Johnston observes, when we sit in prayer, "the very highest form of human energy is brought into play, a human energy that is nothing other than love at the core of one's being. It is precisely this that builds the earth.*

4. *It would seem that the discoveries of contemporary science present us with realities that fundamentally challenge dualistic restrictions that, up to now, limited our view of service to the strict realm of public action preferably with measurable success. If*

simply being can be transformative and helps open the channels for grace, the "ministry of being" can be a very real and viable possibility, and the notion of "call" expands as well.

5. *Authentic community is as wide as the cosmos groaning for redemption. "Our awakening," John of the Cross reminds us, "is an awakening of God, and our uprising is an uprising of God," to which Willigis Jäger adds: "the awakening of society is an awakening of God in society. The awakening of the cosmos is an awakening of God in the evolution of the cosmos."*

6. *"Life itself is a call," my dearest friend told me as she was wrestling with the ever more debilitating effects of cancer moving her toward death. "You go through it, and its terrors turn to opportunities for grace. Cancer too is an event that takes us into God. Life gets thinner, less cluttered, when one experiences serious illness and suffering. One's priorities change and get fewer. The veil becomes more transparent. Being with whatever is will lead us into depths totally unknown."*

7. *A physics that discovers reality as interlaced and interwoven, that discovers the presence*

*of the whole in each part and each part con-
nected to every other part, that sees mind
and matter as, in fact, inextricably linked
with each part of the universe, containing, in
some sense, the entire universe, challenges a
metaphysics of exclusion and triumphalism
to its very core by the utter and uncompromising relationality that it presents as
foundational to all of reality.*

8. *If the whole is in the part, no one with whom
   I minister or for whom I pray, no one I
   think about, in fact, and not even the person
   I do not think about is separate from me,
   from my interiority, from my brokenness,
   and from my redemption, nor is the cosmos whose transformation I am about, nor
   is the God to whom I pray. If interconnectedness — at-onement, is the fabric of reality as
   a whole, we cannot stand apart from one another in any way or for any reason and still
   be authentic ourselves.*

9. *If being is transformative, the call to authenticity can no longer be merely an exhortation
   to personal holiness but speaks, in fact,
   of cosmic ramifications. Baptism (and its
   extension especially into Eucharist, Holy
   Orders, Confirmation, and Matrimony) becomes within this perspective a dynamic*

event that takes "being grafted into the Christ" literally — seeing the Christ event as the creative outpouring of God to which we, as "creation come to consciousness," belong in the most intimate expression of love.

10. *If it is true that "all things and all moments touch each other at every point," then all of us can say and can experience that we partake truly, beyond space and time, in the Christ energy incarnate historically in Jesus of Nazareth. It flows through us who are, in fact, nonlocally and nontemporally connected to Him. It permeates our flesh, as well as our spirits — living signs of the God of our longing, sacraments for the healing and wholeness of the world toward the Christification of the universe.*

IV

Through a Glass Darkly

About a month before Clare died I was asked
to give several lectures on the topic of "Images
of God for Our Time." It is a strange experience to be with someone whose dying presents so
powerful an encounter with stillness that, without uttering a single word, she helps everyone
around her enter the depth mystery and wonder that is God, and then to have to lecture
on the need of images, of names, of relevant
speech that will help make the Holy One present.
Speaking about God can easily run into "the
mortal danger of unconscious piety," says Petru
Dumitriu. His words kept "nudging" me during my preparation: "As soon as one speaks of
God, one manipulates, not one's being, but the
verbal signals which make allusions to [God]."
Manipulation means mastery and excludes piety,
he writes and then suggests that "speaking can
only be reconciled with the love of God *at the
very limit of thought and all its acrobatics.*"[1]
Nevertheless, both encounters with the divine —

the stillness that embraced Clare and permeated her room and a reverent struggle for words and names for the Holy — though strikingly different, are necessary. Both, I believe, can point to the Light, though one goes the way of "uncluttering," hinted at in the preceding essay; the other goes the way of words.

We live in an age where the hunger for God seems particularly acute even if it is ignored or denied by most, where old names and images of God seem to fail us, and new names seem inadequate. The philosopher Martin Heidegger said it well, in his own day (though, I believe, somewhat ahead of his time) when he observed that the gods have fled and we as a human family have not as yet discovered God, have, in fact, not as yet even moved into the space where God can truly reveal God's self.[2] The intensity of our need for God, hidden though it may be for many in countless denials and addictions of every kind, has really nothing to do with true absence. It has, rather, everything to do with our hunger for, yet our *unawareness* of, God's abiding love. These, indeed, are times of great longing, and because the pain has become so unbearable for so many of us, it forces us out of our blindness, or perhaps even the stupor of our indifference, and awakens us to our destiny. Christopher Fry tells us in his *A Sleep of Prisoners,*

Thank God our time is now,
when wrong
Comes up to face us everywhere,
Never to leave us till we take
The longest stride of soul [we humans] ever
    took.
Affairs are now soul size.
The enterprise
Is exploration into God.

Two Stories

Perhaps nothing helps focus the search for God
and identify the reason for our contemporary
blindness and hunger better than a little "tongue
in cheek" vignette told by Armand M. Nigro,
S.J., some years back and used in numerous re-
treats and reflection groups ever since precisely
for this reason. Nigro tells of a rare opportunity
he imagined for himself — a chance to spend one
hour with Jesus. The invitation had come from
Jesus. It was, so we find out, his hope to spend
some time with Nigro in his room — just being together, looking out of the window at the scenery,
and enjoying each other's company. Nigro, on the
other hand, was anticipating this meeting as an
opportunity to receive a major private revelation
from Jesus — useful information about his divinity, his time on earth, his personal thoughts on

the state of his church: " ... for days I prepared by boning up on my seminary course in Christology and I reread the documents of Vatican II. I glanced over my notes on Lonergan's *Method in Theology*, read the latest work on process theology and breezed through another on liberation theology. After all, I didn't want to seem too far out of it." Jesus sensed Nigro's desire to get involved in theological technicalities. He knew well the nervousness and stress that often accompany the need to acquire knowledge that others do not have and to shine as a result. He gently told him to relax: "I just want to be here with you and enjoy the scenery from your window."

For Nigro this seemed incomprehensible. He saw himself as a busy man and surmised Jesus to be infinitely more so. He wanted to deal with the important questions of the day:

"Lord," I broke the silence, "where do you stand on the Christological controversy on how humanly conscious you were of your divinity and future life before your death and resurrection?"

"What's that got to do with our enjoying this scenery together?" he asked.

More silence. I was uneasy. I reached for the book on process theology and said: "He

really has something here on the development of consciousness and the. . . . "

"What difference does it make," he broke
in, "to our time together here? Do you
like the way my Father has fashioned those
clouds in process and the flowing river?"

More silence. I opened the book on liberation theology. "How can your gospel be
authentically proclaimed, Lord, to people
enslaved by oppressive economic and social
structures?"

"You haven't forgiven your brother down
the hall yet, nor let me heal your anger and
unkind judgments of him, have you?" He
countered.

"That doesn't answer my question, Lord."

"Your question does nothing to our pre-
cious time together except mess it up."

More silence.

"Are you happy with Vatican II and the
aftermath of it, Lord?"

"Are you?" he returned.

"Oh, yes, some of the new thinking and
changes are really good, but I think some of
the liberals have carried things too far and
some of the far-right conservatives are ob-
structive and not thinking with the church."

"You are impossible," he laughed. "Aren't
you happy to spend a few friendly minutes

with me without trying to get some new insights for your lousy — I mean brilliant —
class lecture?"

"You're confusing me, Lord. I was taught
how to meditate thirty-four years ago in the
novitiate. And I've studied ever since. I'm not
exactly new at this you know."

"No, not new — just a bit slow — and
dumb. But I love you anyway."

That helped — but not much.

More silence. I saw the shelf I forgot to
dust and a letter that had to be answered and
a message to return a phone call. I thought
of the next class I needed to prepare. I was
getting more restless. . . .

"Do you love me?" he asked.

"Lord, you know everything. You know
that I love you."

"I liked that when Peter said it," he
chided. "But is it really you?"

"Honestly," I protested, "honestly, you're
not making this hour very easy for me."

"You're the one who is making it hard,"
he replied. "I just like to spend time with
you, sharing my presence with you and as-
suring you of my love. You don't ever have
to entertain me when we are together. Just
be there, okay?"

More silence. "Who do you say I am?" he asked, nudging my shoulder.

"Well, I'm with the best of our theologians, Lord, who say that you are — you are the eschatological manifestation of the ground of our being; you are the incarnate word of God; you are our ultimate kerygma and the full revelation of the Trinitarian, Christological, soteriological, antithetic, and ecclesial mysteries of our lives."

There was a long pause before he said, "What?"

Then he exploded with laughter, rose, and raised his arms high up with his head back, roaring.

He gave me a big bear hug.

"You are impossible! But I still love you."

And he left, still laughing all the way down the hall.

I didn't think that was very funny at all.

I stood gazing out the window for a few moments, still confused, before getting back to the important things on a desk full of work.

Then I really missed him.[3]

The hunger for God in our time! What is it, that it touches, consciously or not, even those who proclaim the Word, who have dedicated their lives to teaching, probing the mysteries, and exploring the meaning and implications of holy scripture, of dogmas and doctrines? Why will it not go away even when declarations of infallibility assure us that we "have the truth," that revelation is final and complete?[4] Perhaps another story, this time from the Hindu tradition, can shed some light on our dilemma. It tells about Rishi Uddalaka Aruneyi, a very wise and holy man, who lived in a hermitage with his wife and little son, Svetaketu.

Uddalaka wanted nothing more than that his son gain a deep knowledge of the Hindu scriptures — the *Vedas* — and then learn to move beyond their mere words into their essence. So when the time was ripe he sent his son to study and serve with another wise teacher.

After many years of intense study Svetaketu returned home. He was now a handsome young man of twenty-four who had learned much and was quite sure of his wisdom and excellence. But his knowledge was, as his father knew, bookish with little sense of the nature of existence as such.

One afternoon when both father and son were resting under the old *peepal* tree, Uddalaka gently asked: "My dear son, tell me what you have learned so far."

"Oh, Father," his son replied with outstretched palms and puffed up chest, "Not only have I learned everything that knowledge can possibly teach, but I have also mastered the arts, the sciences, and philosophies."

"Is that so, my son?" his father replied, "Then tell me! Have you sought that knowledge through which the unheard becomes heard, the unthought becomes thought, and the unknown becomes known?"

Listening to that single question, Svetaketu realized the severe limitations of his acquired knowledge and humbly asked his father for further instructions.

The next day his father took Svetaketu to various shops in the city, including a pottery shop with many different vessels for sale. Uddalaka showed his son that all the different vessels, no matter what shape, size, or name, came from a lump of clay. He did the same in a goldsmith shop — showing his son that all things there had originated from a lump of gold. Iron things, he showed him, came from a lump of iron.

As he took his son home, Uddalaka repeated their discovery: "As things made of clay can be known by knowing a lump of clay, as things made of gold can be known by knowing a lump of gold, as things made of iron can be known by knowing a lump of iron, so should one seek that Reality, that essence, which pervades the whole of the universe."

When he saw how eager his son now was to hear about this Reality, he asked him to pick a large piece of fruit from a *nyagrodha* tree. He told him to break the fruit open and tell him what was within. "There are many seeds within," the son replied. His father then asked him to break open the seed. "What is within?" asked the father. Svetaketu looked into the seed and discovered that there was nothing inside.

"Nothing?" his father asked.

"Yes, nothing," Svetaketu replied.

"Hmm! There is nothing inside the seed!" repeated Uddalaka. "Yet, it is from this nothingness that this mighty tree has come into being. So you see, it is this very nothingness, this invisible and subtle essence, which pervades the whole universe. You are that, my son! And that is the Reality."[5]

In his book *The Hidden Heart of the Cosmos*, Brian Swimme, here from a scientist's point of view, also invites us to encounter the no-thing from which everything comes and in which everything is held. He tells us to imagine absolute vacuum — total emptiness, or what scientists call "pure space" — in which no particles, not even the tiniest photons of light, are present. As we imagine this pure space between our cupped hands, he suggests that quantum physicists have discovered that in this absolute nothing

elementary particles ultimately emerge and appear again. He asks us to accept that out of
emptiness everything that is emerges.[6] Diarmuid
O'Murchu says this well in his book *Reclaiming Spirituality:* "What we now realize is that
emptiness is in fact a fullness,...that continuously potentiates, begets, and holds the entire
universal creative process in being....Emptiness
is the precondition for the fullness of life in the
universe."[7]

Approaching the Holy

There are in our tradition two major movements
of what might simply be called "God-encounter,"
two ways, in other words, that seekers of God
have used from the beginning to approach the
Holy One. The first is called *apophatic,* the
second, *cataphatic.*

All of us are familiar with the second way, for it
is, in fact, this one that has us crave for "images
of God in our time." I have discussed both ap-
proaches in my book *Prayer and the Quest for
Healing.* What may bear repeating here, however,
to help focus our reflection is that the cataphatic
approach to spirituality helps us respond to our
own embodied presence, to each other, to the tangible and visible reality around us, and through
them to the Holy permeating the world in which

we live. It gives itself to articulated prayer — to singing, dancing, art, and color; to the writing of psalms, the creating of prayer services, the preparing of liturgies. It calls us to praise, to give thanks, and to mourn. The cataphatic takes the path of language and of symbols. It *speaks* the truths for which the human heart yearns. It writes about them and defines them and proclaims them. Ultimately, it is the reason for holy scripture and for the dogmas and the doctrines that try to communicate and explain its mysteries and wisdom.

In a very strange and mysterious way, however, this cataphatic approach, as important as it is, cannot be authentic without the other, without the apophatic approach on which it, if it is true to itself, is in fact based and in which it is grounded.

Authentic *word* comes from silence, just as being comes out of no-thingness — out of emptiness. The apophatic approach to God comes first. It is primary (even if we get to it sometimes only late in life), because it recognizes the limitations in human symbols, the inadequacy of names, the exaggeration of *all* definitive statements wherever the divine is concerned. It emphasizes the importance of "unknowing" — of the letting go of all assumptions, presuppositions, and expectations whenever we approach the Holy One.

"I pray to God to rid me of God," says Meister

Eckhart and expresses by that his desire to be liberated from all the images that tend to absolutize themselves because of our need for the tangible, for the certain. Eckhart wants to be freed from the glib assurances of his mind and ·its concepts and expectations, its propositions and theories. He wants to be vulnerable, to be poor, to accept his own inherent finitude and incapacity in the face of the Holy. He wants to let God open him up, heal him. For in the event of healing, as Heidegger recognized many years later, the Holy is *called forth:* The recognition and agony of *absence* makes *present,* Heidegger says. The Holy, which in this way shines forth, lays hold in turn on divinity whose atmosphere, if you will, can then allow for the approach of God.[8] The apophatic disposition requires "vacuum." It is a condition of complete emptiness, because it is in emptiness — in total stillness above all — that God can be encountered.

It is clear that we are facing a paradox here in our approach to God that can perhaps best be identified as follows: For human interaction and communication images and words are essential, but human images and words are never adequate and (taken by themselves) can, in fact, be totally misleading. Authentic words emerge out of silence and move back into silence. The apophatic recognition of human limitations in the face of God provides for us the environment in which cataphatic song and praise can flourish and then, in their turn, deepen once more the stillness whence they came.

We are today — through the discoveries of science, which I have mentioned throughout this book — more aware than ever of the *mystery* of reality. Scientists, at times perhaps more so than theologians, have in our age spoken to the mystical dimension of reality and embraced it. They caution against arrogance in our approach to our world: against the notion that ultimately dominion of the world is ours, against the illusion of limitless knowledge. Physicist Louis de Broglie speaks of the need for a "supplement of soul" in the scientific inquiry into the nature of reality. He suggests an "ontological order which is beyond us":

> Mystery surrounds us. . . . We are placed as at the centre of a small clearing surrounded on all sides by an immense . . . unexplored forest. No, it is not yet tomorrow that science will be able to give us the keys to the enigmas of the universe; we are not yet near to the attainment of the end of an effort to which nothing permits us to fix the duration.[9]

Sir Arthur Eddington in his "Defense of Mysticism" says it boldly:

Call it of God, of the devil, fanaticism, un-
reason, but do not underrate the power of
the mystic. . . .

Scientific instincts warn me that any attempt to answer the question "What is real?"
in a broader sense than that adopted for do-
mestic purposes in science, is likely to lead
to a floundering among vain words and high-
sounding epithets. We all know that there are
regions of the human spirit untrammelled
by the world of physics. In the mystic sense
of the creation around us, in the expression of art, in a yearning towards God, the
soul grows upward and finds the fulfillment
of something implanted in its nature. The
sanction for this development is within us,
a striving born with our consciousness or an
Inner Light proceeding from a greater power
than ours. . . . Whether in the intellectual pursuits of science or in the mystical pursuits of
the spirit, the light beckons ahead and the
purpose surging in our nature responds.[10]

In our approach to God, the "science" of theology,
i.e., clear-cut language, metaphysical definitions,
and ultimately unalterable dogmas and doctrines,
needs, I believe, to take seriously the unfath-
omable mystery of the Holy as well or become
less and less helpful. Karl Rahner had it right:

> The concepts and words which we use [are] *merely* the tiny signs and idols which we erect and *have to* erect so that they constantly remind us of the... *silently offered* ... and *graciously silent experience* of... the mystery in which, in spite of all the light offered by the everyday awareness of things, we reside, *as if in a dark night* and a *pathless wilderness.*

And later on in the same essay entitled "Experiencing the Spirit":

> In this unnamed and unsignposted expanse of our consciousness there dwells that which we call God. The mystery pure and simple that we call God is not a special, particularly unusual piece of objective reality, something to be added to and included in the other realities of our naming and classifying experience. [God] is the comprehensive though never comprehended ground and presupposition of our experience and of the objects of that experience.[11]

Standing in the Tension

Now, the speaking about God that respects the silence and humility necessary for an authentic approach to the Mystery; the speaking, in other words, that acknowledges its own inadequacy while recognizing, at the same time, our need for communication; the speaking that admits the similarity and at the same time the dissimilarity — the "is" and at the same time the "is not" of every name given to the Holy and every word spoken about our encounter with the Holy, might perhaps best be described as metaphor. What I am suggesting is that all authentic language about God, all naming and all helpful images of the Mystery that is God are of necessity analogical.

Metaphor helps us navigate the tension of the "is" and the "is not" that authentic encounter with God always evokes. If this tension is respected, it can help us touch depth reality that we cannot otherwise reach. But precisely because of this tension and our discomfort with it, we are ever tempted to ignore the essentially metaphoric approach that God-talk necessitates and to come down either on the side of the "is," or on the side of the "is not." This, of course, destroys the metaphor and shuts out the depth it opens up for us. We either cheapen it or we *literalize* it.[12]

The great danger in God-language is literalization. We speak, for example, of God as our Father. This clearly is a powerful metaphor that points to the creative energy of the all-caring love that Jesus experienced in God and passed on to us. All of us would surely agree, however, that it has nothing to do with the literal generation of offspring through sexual intercourse. God is neither a male being nor engages in sexual intercourse. Nor, as Sandra Schneiders so well points out, is God *literally* our adoptive Father.[13] That too is a metaphor. Literalization happens when we suppress the "is not" of the metaphoric tension, and identify with the symbol used. That this has happened with the "fatherhood" of God is beyond debate. One has only to attend the liturgical functions of most Christian churches or listen to the absolutist declarations of their official teachings to experience the impoverishment and exclusivism that this has brought about.

But, if God is not literally a father, God also is not literally a mother, or a friend, or a fortress, or a dove, or an eagle, or a fiery flame, or a king with a kingdom, or a Lord, or a lamb. The metaphors we have used to speak about God say something about God, but they cannot be equated with God.

We all know this, of course. In a way, it is merely common sense. Yet, strangely, many of us still smile with embarrassment and, quite likely, still feel ill at ease when we hear someone use a feminine parental metaphor for God. We know that our church's magisterial administration actually forbids us to do so in the official lectionaries of our tradition, and that, in itself, is for many (even if they do not consciously admit it) a power-

ful deterrent to deeper thought on this issue.
Somehow we want to eradicate the "is not" from
our traditional God-language even if, deep down,
we know that we can't, and so we objectify or absolutize one side of the metaphor in the hope that
the other side will disappear.

Literalization causes the cataphatic to loose its
grounding in the apophatic. When that happens,
it tries to stand on its own validity, and that is
when religion becomes trite. We act, then, says
Karl Rahner, as if we could slap God on the
shoulder, as if we were God's supervisors or God's
equals.[14] Metaphors are used in religious language, Sandra Schneiders suggests, because our
mind is incapable of finding a "literal way to ex-
press something that demands expression," but
cannot be translated except through the tension
of the "is" and "is not."[15]

There is something truly liberating when one
allows oneself the freedom to let go of compul-
sory religious language. Many of us have done
so, and for the educated believer what I have reflected on is certainly nothing new. The matter
becomes a bit more complex, however, when one
explores some of the theological "derivatives"
that are rooted in absolutized religious language
and present us with what may be a more painful
"is not."

Perhaps the fatherhood of God could, once

again, serve as an example here: Through Jesus we experience God as loving, nurturing, caring, and protecting, and with him we call this experience "Father." (Let us "bracket" for the moment that many of us because of the context of our time have been liberated sufficiently to call this experience "Mother" as well.) Christian faith has chosen the "Father" metaphor because our experience of God comes closest to, and therefore can be expressed best in terms of, the human nurturance of a good parent. So, for us, God *is* Father and, of course, also *is not* any of that which is associated with physical parenting.

Now in the light of our considerations it may be easy to nod our heads here and even to dismiss the above as something we already know. But what of religious teachings that build on this metaphor while they seem to ignore its metaphoric dimension? What, for example, of "virgin birth," what of "conceived of the Holy Spirit," and what of the divinity of Jesus when it is connected to his conception without an earthly father? Is there a literal "divine seed" implanted into Mary whose human ovum must be ignored? And if so, where does this (physical) "divine seed" come from? Do we as Christians of today seriously wish to remain in a belief system based, consciously or not, on medieval biology, which was, in fact, only familiar with the father's seed and had no idea of the mother's part in procreation?* If we do, can we, with our present-day knowledge of biology, of what is involved in procreation, and with our experience also of surrogate childbearing, accept that Mary really is the "mother" of Jesus? Or is she for us now simply the "vessel" — the womb that bore him? If we reject this kind of reasoning, how do we understand the divinity of Jesus beyond its biological moorings? These are upsetting questions. They can be scoffed at by sophisticates, but the average Christian, and certainly our youth looking for meaning in their faith, cannot ignore them that easily. Literalization does havoc with depth faith. Our concern as authentic believers must, I believe, always be to nurture the depth. For this the "is not" of religious metaphor has to be addressed, however, with respect and candor.

Honoring the Silence

It seems to me that what we need to appreciate if we are to overcome these difficulties is that human self-expression through language, instead of being merely an "objective pointing to a specific reality," is primarily a "medium of encounter" with depth. It is first and foremost a

*The ovum as necessary for procreation was discovered only in 1827.

way by which we open ourselves up to each other and to the world, "a mutual entering into interiority," as Sandra Schneiders puts it. "Language is used for self-expression before it is used for the communication of neutral information," she says.[16] And because of this, language is primarily symbolic and only very secondarily technical and objective. And because of this, also, we can use language to name God.

Symbols are used to "presence" something that cannot otherwise be encountered. Such a "presencing" is thwarted when the symbolic character of language is reduced to the merely technical and objective — when Mary's virginity, for example, is reduced to an intact hymen, or Jesus' divinity becomes dependent, literally, on divine paternity.[17] A symbol makes perceptible what without it remains imperceptible.[18] It draws the perceptible and imperceptible together. It points beyond itself into depth and makes the latter visible.

It seems to me that in the light of the above and the technical reductionism it invites us to let go of, the *depth* of Virgin Motherhood can be beautifully retrieved. Mary was and is *Virgin,* I suggest, in the most profound and sacred sense of that word, where the biological issue is indeed a nonissue. The hollowness of a virgin's womb *symbolizes her entire being.* She was, indeed, the empty space, the open vulnerability of Carol Houselander's "Reed of God." Into her openness, and because of her openness, God's silent, overwhelming presence could manifest itself. Her emptiness became the place, the home, for this presence. Her character, her disposition, not any physical condition, was the foundation for her motherhood. Mary, thus, becomes the archetype, the root symbol of human freedom as surrender to God — a freedom, as was discussed in the previous chapter, not so much of action as of being, a freedom that makes the presence of the Divine possible and, therefore, gives God to the world. "Mary's 'yes,' " I have written elsewhere,

> was made possible by the freedom in which she was held. Her being *as surrendered,* if you will, was the precondition for the act of consent. In a deeper than biological sense, she was Mother (the virgin mother [that the mystical soul hungers to be]) *before* the spoken fiat; and, because she was *who she was,* the Mystery could unfold in her consent and become fruit.[19]

And because she was who she was — human in the most authentic sense of the word — we too can walk in her footsteps and, as the mystic Eckhart would have us, also become virgin mothers: so empty and so free that God can breathe through us too — over and over again into this world, yes, into this universe, toward ever deeper Christification. The depth symbol of virginity, thus, is multivalent and touches us all.

But when a symbol is forced to remain within its own literal boundaries and is not allowed the freedom of the tension between the "is" and the "is not," its depth purpose is aborted. Its interiority is destroyed. Its symbolic power dies. We start worrying, then, about whether Mary had a husband and other children, whether the Holy Spirit implanted his seed and, therefore, would have to be male because Jesus, after all, was a man. With this, religion loses its mooring in the sacred, becomes laughable, and all of us are impoverished.

The metaphoric use of symbol is among the most powerful modalities of religious expression. It is tragic when metaphors become trite, banal, and lose their power. I do believe that we live in a time when our awareness of this is becoming sharpened. Our sense of history and historical context, of the evolution of consciousness and human self-understanding, of the democratic right to self-expression and the importance of true discernment all have contributed to our freedom to search for meaning, to ask the relevant questions, perhaps to remain for a long time with the question without need for an im-

mediate answer, and, thus, to move courageously
beyond bland explanations into depth.

Of late an old German evening song keeps
"singing itself" in my memory and haunts me
with the simplicity of its lyrics. In its own gentle
way it calls attention to the mystery that graces
all of reality and reminds me of what Heidegger would call the "with-holding" that pervades
every revelation and stirs our deepest longing.
The song draws our attention to the evening sky,
to the moon and the magnificent array of stars.
It sings of the forest that stands silently in the
dark of the night, and of the fog that rises gently over the meadows. It whispers of the stillness
that pervades the once busy world, and then,
once again, it turns our attention to the moon —
that mysterious and silent visitor of the night
sky whose one side is ever hidden from us. So
too, the song tells us, it is with much of reality,
the many events of our life that we assume to
understand and about which we may even laugh
because our eyes, indeed, are barred from *truly
seeing*.[20] Paul, it seems to me, was right, and we
forget his exhortation only at our own peril and
impoverishment:

> For now we see in a mirror dimly [the New
> Jerusalem Bible adds: "mere riddles"], but
> then we see face to face." (1 Cor. 13:12)

Thoughts and Questions for Meditation

What are your thoughts concerning the following selections from chapter 4?

1. *The intensity of our need for God, hidden though it may be for many in countless denials and addictions of every kind, has really nothing to do with true absence. It has, rather, everything to do with our hunger for, yet our unawareness of, God's abiding love.*

2. *The hunger for God in our time! ... Why will it not go away even when declarations of infallibility assure us that we "have the truth," that revelation is final and complete?*

3. *So you see, it is this very nothingness, this invisible and subtle essence, which pervades the whole universe. You are that, my son! And that is the Reality.... "What we now realize is that emptiness is in fact a fullness ... that continuously potentiates, begets, and holds the entire universal creative process in being.... Emptiness is the precondition for the fullness of life in the universe."*

4. *Authentic word comes from silence, just as being comes out of no-thingness — out of emptiness. The apophatic approach to God comes first. It is primary (even if we get to it sometimes only late in life), because it recog-*

nizes the limitations in human symbols, the inadequacy of names, the exaggeration of all definitive statements wherever the divine is concerned. It emphasizes the importance of "unknowing" — of the letting go of all assumptions, presuppositions, expectations, whenever we approach the Holy One.

5. *Metaphor helps us navigate the tension of the "is" and the "is not" that authentic encounter with God always evokes. If this tension is respected, it can help us touch depth reality that we cannot otherwise reach. But precisely because of this tension and our discomfort with it, we are ever tempted to ignore the essentially metaphoric approach that God-talk necessitates and to come down either on the side of the "is," or on the side of the "is not." This, of course, destroys the metaphor and shuts out the depth it opens up for us. We either cheapen it or we literalize it.*

6. *But, if God is not literally a father, God also is not literally a mother, or a friend, or a fortress, or a dove, or an eagle, or a fiery flame, or a king with a kingdom, or a Lord, or a lamb. The metaphors we have used to speak about God say something about God, but they cannot be equated with God. In a way, it is merely common sense. Yet, strangely,*

many of us still feel ill at ease when we hear someone use a feminine parental metaphor for God. We know that our Church's magisterial administration actually forbids us to do so in the official lectionaries of our tradition, and that, in itself, is for many a powerful deterrent to deeper thought on this issue.

7. *Symbols are used to "presence" something that cannot otherwise be encountered. Such a "presencing" is thwarted when the symbolic character of language is reduced to the merely technical and objective — when Mary's virginity, for example, is reduced to an intact hymen, or Jesus' divinity becomes dependent, literally, on divine paternity.*

8. *Mary was and is Virgin, I suggest, in the most profound and sacred sense of that word, where the biological issue is indeed a non-issue. The hollowness of a virgin's womb symbolizes her entire being. She was, indeed, the empty space, the open vulnerability of Carol Houselander's "Reed of God." Into her openness, and because of her openness, God's silent, overwhelming presence could manifest itself. Her emptiness became the place, the home, for this presence. Her character, her disposition, not any physical condition, was the foundation for her motherhood.*

V

*For I Have Set You
an Example*

In 1958 a British man (S.B.), blind since he was
ten months old, received cornea transplants. He
was fifty years of age at the time of the surgery
and was rejoicing in the fact that for the first time
in his life, he would have the proper tools for seeing. Yet, in spite of perfectly functioning eyes and
to his bitter disappointment, he remained unable
to see. Blurs, where he should have been able to
identify faces, were all he could make out. He
struggled for sight until he died a few years later
but never managed to overcome the inner bar-
rier that resisted this new faculty for information
and ever referred him back to the tried and true
vehicles of touch and sound.

S.B.'s case is not the only one. "During a critical window in the first years of life," Arthur
Zajonc, who tells this story in his book *Catching the Light,* points out, "visual as well as many
other sensory and motor skills such as speech
and walking are formed. If this opportunity is

missed, trying to make up for it at a later time is enormously difficult and mostly unsuccessful."[1] It would seem that the functional physical organ of the eye depends on what Zajonc calls "an inner light" for the gift of sight. This inner light, the light of our mind, is acquired through education — the formation of visual imagination. Once our habits of contact with reality, *our relational tools,* are developed, we resist new ones even if they are better and more suitable for the task. "New impressions threaten the security of a world previously built upon the sensations of touch and hearing," Zajonc observes. "Some decide it is better to be blind in their own world than sighted in an alien one."[2]

It is not difficult to intuit an interesting analogy opened up for us by this 1958 event. Structures of perception, as we all know, go far beyond mere physical sight. Habits of every kind of interpretation and belief can be as intransigent as the mental processes for physical sight. This very likely is true of many of the issues we have been pondering in the earlier chapters of this book and is perhaps particularly painful in this age of paradigm shifts and collapsing worldviews. Cultures can easily resist change when their values and interpretations are threatened and can engage in all sorts of subterfuge to hide their resistance. Religions can do so as well, especially when the views

that are threatened by the new outlook have previously been canonized as permanently revealed
by God.

We reflected on the literalized metaphor of religious language in chapter 4 and stressed how
important it is for a viable religious perspective
to resist excessive intellectualization and unnec-
essary dogmatism in order to allow room for the
mystery. But modes of behavior, cultural taboos,
and rituals as well as the meaning derived from
them also can succumb to blindness or to an unwillingness on our part to look deeper. Were not
the struggles Jesus encountered in his day largely
due to the resistance of those whom he would
have healed?

> For this people's heart has grown dull,
> and their ears are hard of hearing,
> and they have shut their eyes;
> so that they might not look with their eyes,
> and listen with their ears,
> and understand with their heart and turn —
> and I would heal them. (Matt. 13:15)

The Foot-washing

I wonder whether in the case of ritual intransigence, it is possible to have "done" something for
so long in a particular way and out of a limited

perspective that it becomes impossible to "see" beyond the parameters of meaning we have set up for ourselves over the years. Might it be then that we, like S.B. and others like him, resist the opportunity for an expansion or deepening of our vision?

Not long ago a friend of mine gave me two prints of paintings by the German artist Sieger Köder. One, entitled *Abendmahl,* depicts the Last Supper. The disciples, rustic and awe-struck, are gathered in the familiar scene around the table. Jesus, seemingly with his back toward the viewer, is holding the bread and the cup. Aside from his hands, he is visible only as a countenance with penetrating eyes reflected in the cup. The painting is unusual in its simplicity and reverence: simple people with simple wonder in their eyes manifesting simple faith. The one who would not or could not "see" is leaving through a dark door in the back of the room.

Somehow, as if by intuition, I had *Abendmahl* matted and framed together with the second print, *Fußwaschung* (Foot-washing). This painting too has Jesus, this time visibly with his back to the viewer, kneeling in front of Peter, who is bending over him with great tenderness. The hands of Jesus are resting on the bucket where we can see his face reflected once again but now in the water. In the background is a table with bread and cup.

I have prayed much over both pictures, especially over my need to see them together in one frame. Sandra Schneiders sees "root metaphors" as religious symbols noted for being particularly capable of evoking both feeling and thought response, as having an endless reservoir of depth and a perennial gift for drawing us forth: "A root metaphor," she says, "like the root system of a tree in relation to the nutrients in the soil, draws together in a living synthesis numerous diverse cognitive and affective elements and nourishes ever new growth in meaning."[3] Clearly the events of the Last Supper fall into the category of "root metaphor," of foundational or "charter" symbol. They connect us to our deepest belonging and speak of who we are as covenant community, as people of God, as witnesses to God's reign.

But what was it that had me juxtapose the prints of Köder's two paintings in a single frame? Was it merely the fact that they were works of the same painter? Was it, perhaps more seriously, that both events took place on the same evening? Or could it be that there really were not two events but only one? And if so, why is it that we remember one with so much fervor, rubrics, and ritual and remember the other peripherally almost and, sometimes even with adapted symbols (the washing of hands instead of feet), only on the Feast of the Last Supper? Do we "see," I wonder, the "charter" connection? Or have years of triumphalism made us incapable of recognizing that the breaking of the bread and the sharing of the cup lose their meaning without the washing of the feet?

We know that the breaking and the sharing of the bread was not a novel act on the part of Jesus, nor was the drinking from a shared cup at the end of the meal. Both activities marked Jewish festive ritual meals and were symbolic of covenant, of the pledge of connectedness as community with each other and with God. What Jesus did, therefore, with his disciples "reflects the pattern of Jewish festive (and Passover) meals."[4] What Jesus *meant*, however, and *implied* by his actions and words, marks the new: " 'This is myself': by sharing this meal with you I am bringing you into an intimate relationship with myself." This is what Jesus meant, so the scripture scholar Jerome Kodell insists: There was a mandate here "to continue doing what Jesus had done."[5] And this, I have come to believe, is what links Köder's two paintings and what their togetherness depicts for me.

The foot-washing was indeed extraordinary and very new, and, even if only John records this event for our edification, its symbolic significance is nevertheless a root issue pointing to our belonging together and to the Christ:

> After he had washed their feet,
> had put on his robe,
> and had returned to the table, he said to them,
> Do you know what I have done to you?
> You call me Teacher and Lord —
> and you are right, for that is what I am.
> So if I, your Lord and Teacher,
> have washed your feet,
> you also ought to wash one another's feet.
> For I have set you an example,
> that you also should do as I have done to you.
>
> (John 13:12–15)

The New Covenant

Who is the Christ whom we remember at the Eucharist, if not, in the deepest sense, what each of us *is meant to be:* a servant of God's reign and, therefore, surrendered to God in love of neighbor? The covenant of the Eucharist, the New Covenant in Christ Jesus, is the commitment, even to the point of death, to God's cause — to the holiness, health, and wholesomeness that blossoms in a society of equals where all are welcome and all are fed around the table of God's justice. The foot-washing represents this commitment in a unique and, yes, in a deeply poignant way. It is the primary symbol, if you will, of the essential equality of the Christian covenant community where the leader is one with the community and models, in fact, the servanthood of all.

It seems to me that the fundamental ethos of the New Covenant that Jesus initiated at his last Passover meal with his followers cannot be ignored if we are truly "to do this," and to do all that we do, "in memory" of him. Have we, however, not sidestepped this issue far too long? Does not our church's excessive emphasis on, and concern around, the "how" of Christ's presence in the Eucharist, around who can preside and who may partake sadly miss the point of the matter? Perhaps the reason why the foot-washing has taken on such primary importance for me when I reflect on all of this is the dissonance I sense between the miters some wear and others envy and the bucket of water in the upper room. Many of us long to connect again to the original intent and to experience covenant where it belongs — in the community gathered in humility and service.

It is interesting to me that Jesus himself was deeply concerned that his followers truly understand and note what he had modeled for them. "Do you know what I have done to you?" he asked them and then explained quite clearly his

intent. Nevertheless, all signs seem to point to
the fact that over the years we have forgotten his
concern, and that our habit of ignoring the depth
implications of servanthood has grown to a blindness of attitude that tends to consider presiding
over ritual behavior as the domain of the chosen few and as an occasion for prestige. We seem
blind to the fact that Christ's presence is primarily connected to the community gathered in love
and justice, and that the ritual formula uttered
by the presider is of itself meaningless without this context. Our memory appears to have
been dulled, and, from my observation of late
twentieth-century ecclesial retrenchment, much
of the effort on the part of scholars and thinkers
to help us regain focus, let alone vision, seems to
have gone for naught. One simply silences them
and then "keeps on keeping on."

It is not as if Jesus had modeled his priorities
only that once at the foot-washing. The entire
purpose of his presence in our midst was one
of liberation and healing, of pointing beyond
himself, of presenting a different, emancipatory,
and neighbor-centered, worldview. "Kyriarchy,"
as Elisabeth Schüssler Fiorenza terms the all-
pervasive insistence on personal prominence and
entitlement, on "overlording" and forcing others
into subservience, was foreign to Jesus. "Kyriar-
chal societies and cultures need a 'servant class.' "

They are, among other things, sustained by the belief that God wills this — some people are inferior, others superior by divine decree.[6] Jesus had no use for such views. He "sought to renew the Jewish people for the reign of [God]." His mission of "solidarity with the poor and the despised, his call into a discipleship of voluntary service," the totality, in fact, of his life and action became "the symbol and model of the full but not yet realized way of being human."[7]

> You know that the rulers of the gentiles
> lord it over them
> and the great make their authority felt.
> It shall not be so with you;
> among you, whoever wants to be great
> must be your servant,
> and whoever wants to be first
> must be the slave of all. (Matt. 20:25–27)

Nowhere, I believe, is Jesus' mission described more clearly than in the vision of the "Palestinian Jesus movement" as described by Schüssler Fiorenza in her book *In Memory of Her:*

> The Palestinian Jesus movement understands the ministry and mission of Jesus as that of the prophet and child of Sophia sent to announce that God is the God of the poor and heavy laden, of the outcasts and those who

suffer injustice. As child of Sophia he stands in a long line and succession of prophets sent to gather the children of Israel to their gracious Sophia-God.

For Jesus the passionate concern of his liberating mission was to make God *real*, to stress the *experience* of God's love, and to form a community where God's vision for humanity would be embraced:

> [The] reality of God-Sophia spelled out in the preaching, healings, exorcisms, and inclusive table community of Jesus called forth a circle of disciples who were to continue what Jesus did. Sophia, the God of Jesus, wills the wholeness and humanity of everyone and therefore enables the Jesus movement to become a "discipleship of equals." They are called to one and the same praxis of inclusiveness and equality lived by Jesus-Sophia. Like Jesus, they are sent to announce to everyone in Israel the presence of the *basileia,* as God's gracious future, among the impoverished, the starving, the tax collectors, sinners, and prostitutes. Like Jesus, his disciples are sent to make the *basileia* experientially available in their healings and exorcisms, by restoring the humanity and wholeness of Sophia-God's children.[8]

This *was* the covenant into which his disciples were officially drawn at their last Passover meal with Jesus when they broke bread and shared the cup. It was symbolized in a unique way by the foot-washing and ratified in their sharing. Their experience of the God of compassion and unconditional love through Jesus and their radical "yes" to this experience, weak and sinful though they were, sealed their membership as a community of inclusion and equality. That was the vision he bequeathed to them. It was the vision and the message symbolized by his entire life, from the moment of his birth in a stable in Bethlehem: God present among the poor, the outcast, the frightened and cold, to his death on the cross: God persecuted and rejected, imprisoned, humiliated, and beaten; God crucified among sinners, forgiving them and loving them into paradise.

In Jesus the symbol and thus the "presencing" of the fullness of God in creation is realized. Our covenant draws us, as it did his followers from the beginning, into this same presence. The God incarnate in Jesus incarnates ever anew in us who are Christ's Body today. God — friend of the poor, liberator of the oppressed, child among children, persecuted among those seeking justice, voice for transformation — is *our* God and can "presence" only in and through us. That is why the foot-washing was so important and why our forgetting or belittling or ignoring it in our time can relegate us, and all those who need the authentic experience of the Holy One through us, to irreparable blindness and despair.

There seemed to be an urgency when Jesus asked the question: "Do you know what I have done to you?" and an urgency also in the explanation that followed. The covenant *depended* on their understanding. Blind acquiescence was not what Jesus wanted of them. His was a message *of* freedom *for* freedom. There could be no compromise here.

I feel that urgency again today. Our covenant in Christ is a sacred but also a fragile trust that can easily be betrayed. It is easy to proclaim ourselves "in possession of the truth" and to demand that others see from our vantage point. It is easy to claim the mantle of "righteousness" and expect others to live by our rules. It is easy to speak our views in the name of God and silence those with whom we do not wish to dialogue. It is easy to claim the ideals of freedom for ourselves but deny them to others. It is easy to live with the "haves" and ignore the "have-nots," to proclaim a "new world order" for one part of the world only. It is easy to exclude as long as we belong, to look "down" on others as long as we are "up." But the Jesus community that, because of the attitude and the entire life of Jesus, had experienced the foot-washing as one with the sharing of bread and cup and could, therefore, not understand one without the other, were cut of a different cloth and saw with different eyes. Theirs was a different ethos, for they had been gathered intentionally from the periphery of their culture and religion. They had been the outcasts and sinners, but they had been found, and they knew it.

> They were those without future, but now they had hope again; they were the "outcast" and marginal people in their society, but now they had community again; they were despised and downtrodden, but now they had dignity and self-confidence as God Sophia's beloved children; they were, because of life's circumstances and social injustices, sinners with no hope to share in the holiness and presence of God, but now they were heirs of the *basileia,* experiencing the gracious goodness of God who had made them equal to the holy and righteous in Israel.[9]

The breaking of the bread and the sharing of the cup of the New Covenant was, and is also today, about commitment and belonging.

- It involved no magic trick, no extraterrestrial power, nor does it today.

- Its power to transform was and continues to be the power of love and fidelity to a cause symbolized in the foot-washing and called "the reign of God."

- It found and continues to find its expression in service, in humility, in acceptance and inclusivity.

- It was and is *here* and also *not yet* and must continue to be realized wherever the community gathers in Christ's name.

Radical Application

The redemptive love of Jesus includes all without exception. He loves the very sinners we despise. And here is perhaps where the covenant we profess has been and is most readily compromised and where the "not yet" is most clearly visible.

I read an interesting reflection not long ago that illustrates this dilemma with unflinching honesty: Ron Ashmore, a priest in Terre Haute, Indiana, in an article written for the *National Catholic Reporter* shortly before the execution of Timothy McVeigh, meditates on Tim's welcome into God's embrace: "McVeigh will meet unimaginable mercy" was the headline introducing his reflection. He writes of his prayer and of the whis-

per of God's love that came to him on the day he
first found out about the bombing:

> In silence I listened. "Those who are dead
> are already with me in the joy and peace of
> the Kingdom. In the embrace of my mercy,
> they have already forgiven the one who killed
> them. They await his arrival to invite him to
> sit down with them for a wonderful meal on
> the holy mountain of God like the prophet
> Isaiah spoke of. He will be surprised, but they
> are waiting for him with love and joy. It will
> take time for their families to realize the im-
> mensity of my love. Their pain, tears, anger,
> vengeful rage do not exist here. Everyone
> came here so quickly, it surprised them. And
> the little children are so happy. They want to
> sit down on his lap and give him a hug. You,
> their families and he can hardly imagine the
> power of God's mercy that is everything here.
> Here, my loving forgiveness makes everyone
> see things in a new way. You and they will
> learn it. Just remember, forgive them."[10]

This message of unconditional love may be difficult to hear when one suffers the loss of a dear
one, violently killed in what appears so senseless
an act as was the bombing in Oklahoma City. We
are a nation where revenge has been "civilized"
as appropriate punishment, where violence in re-

sponse to violence is seen as justice. The Christian message has been customized accordingly. It is difficult to recover from this blindness and regain one's sight. Yet radical honesty gives us no choice. Whether we like it or not, forgiveness, not revenge, is the Christian mandate. Julian of Norwich, reflecting on her "showings," says it well:

> Holy Church taught me that sinners are sometimes worthy of blame and wrath, but I could not see these in God in my showing. I saw that our Lord was never wrathful, nor ever shall be. God's lucidity and unity will not allow this. God is the goodness that cannot be wrathful.[11]

And again:

> I saw no kind of vengeance in God, not for a short time nor for long. . . . I knew by the common teaching of Holy Church and by my own feeling that the blame for our sins clings to us continually while we are on this earth. How amazing it was then to see . . . God showing us no more blame than if we were as clean and whole as the Angels in heaven.[12]

The gospel exhortations agree with Julian. Forgiveness is a constant theme practiced by Jesus until his last breath.

It might help to "even things out" somewhat in this discussion on the forgiveness, acceptance, and inclusion of all modeled for us *as God's* by Christ Jesus and demanded by the radical nature of Eucharistic Christianity, if we allow ourselves to focus also on our *own* littleness, *our* brokenness, and *our* wounds. This, Brennan Manning points out, is indeed "crucial to the evangelical enterprise." And, although forgiveness of one's self would have to follow but is not at all easy, our recognition that we also need mercy may at least help open the door for us to the experience of solidarity with our sisters and brothers. "It is not 'they' who are poor, sinful and lost. It is ourselves," says Brennan Manning. "Unless we acknowledge that we are the sinners, the sick ones and the lost sheep for whom Jesus came," he insists, "we do not belong to the 'blessed' who know that they are poor and inherit the kingdom. Solidarity with human suffering frees the one who receives and liberates the one who gives through the conscious awareness 'I am the other.' "[13] With this recognition, comparative concepts such as higher and lower, worthy and unworthy, noble and ignoble, virtuous and sinful simply cease to make sense.

The symbol of the Eucharist, not just on that last day before Jesus died but in meals and gatherings throughout his life — with publicans and sinners, with the important and the little people, with women and men — stands for unity and reconciliation. It testifies without exception to the great belonging and to the great responsibility that such communion requires. In it our oneness with each other as Christ's Body is sealed.

> If you want to know what is the body of Christ, hear what the Apostle tells believers: "You are Christ's body and his members" (1 Cor 12:27). If, then, you are Christ's body and his members, it is your symbol that lies on the Lord's altar — what you receive is a symbol of yourself. When you say "Amen" to what you are, your saying it affirms it. You hear [the priest say] "The body of Christ," and you answer "Amen," and you must *be* the body of Christ to make that "Amen" take effect.   — Augustine[14]

Thoughts and Questions for Meditation

What are your thoughts concerning the following selections from chapter 5?

1. *This inner light, the light of our mind, is acquired through education — the formation of visual imagination. Once our habits of contact with reality, our relational tools, are developed, we resist new ones even if they are better and more suitable for the task. "New impressions threaten the security of a world previously built upon the sensations of touch and hearing," Zajonc observes. "Some decide it is better to be blind in their own world than sighted in an alien one."*

2. *I wonder whether in the case of ritual intransigence, it is possible to have "done" something for so long in a particular way and out of a limited perspective that it becomes impossible to "see" beyond the parameters of meaning we have set up for ourselves over the years. Might it be then that we resist the opportunity for an expansion of our vision?*

3. *Have years of triumphalism made us incapable of recognizing that the breaking of the bread and the sharing of the cup lose their meaning without the washing of the feet?*

4. *We know that the breaking and the sharing of the bread was not a novel act on the part of Jesus, nor was the drinking from a shared cup at the end of the meal. What Jesus did with his disciples "reflects the pattern of Jewish festive (and Passover) meals." What Jesus meant, however, and implied by his actions and words, marks the new: " 'This is myself': by sharing this meal with you I am bringing you into an intimate relationship with myself." There was a mandate here "to continue doing what Jesus had done." And this, I have come to believe, is what links Köder's two paintings and what their togetherness depicts.*

5. *Who is the Christ whom we remember at the Eucharist, if not, in the deepest sense, what each of us is meant to be: a servant of God's reign and, therefore, surrendered to God in love of neighbor? The covenant of the Eucharist, the New Covenant in Christ Jesus, is the commitment, even to the point of death, to God's cause — to the holiness, health, and wholesomeness that blossoms in a society of equals where all are welcome and all are fed around the table of God's justice.*

6. *The foot-washing represents this commitment in a unique, and yes, in a deeply*

poignant way. It is the primary symbol, if you will, of the essential equality of the Christian covenant community where the leader is one with the community and models, in fact, the servanthood of all.

7. *Perhaps the reason why the foot-washing has taken on such primary importance for me when I reflect on all of this is the dissonance I sense between the miters some wear and others envy and the bucket of water in the upper room. Many of us long to connect again to the original intent and to experience covenant where it belongs — in the community gathered in humility and service.*

8. *In Jesus the symbol and thus the "presencing" of the fullness of God in creation is realized. Our covenant draws us, as it did his followers from the beginning, into this same presence. The God incarnate in Jesus incarnates ever anew in us who are Christ's Body today. God — friend of the poor, liberator of the oppressed, child among children, persecuted among those seeking justice, voice for transformation — is our God and can "presence" only in and through us. That is why the foot-washing was so important and why our forgetting or belittling or ignoring it in our time can relegate us, and all those who*

*need the authentic experience of the Holy
One through us, to irreparable blindness and
despair.*

9. *The redemptive love of Jesus includes all
without exception. He loves the very sinners
we despise. And here is perhaps where the
covenant we profess has been and is most
readily compromised and where the "not
yet" of God's reign is most clearly visible.*

10. *The symbol of the Eucharist, not just on that
last day before Jesus died but in meals and
gatherings throughout his life — with publicans and sinners, with the important and
the little people, with women and men —
stands for unity and reconciliation. It testifies without exception to the great belonging
and to the great responsibility that such communion requires. In it our oneness with each
other as Christ's Body is sealed.*

VI

Blessed Are Those Who Mourn

Nothing can fill the gap when we are away
from those we love, and it would be wrong
to try and find anything. We must simply
hold out.... That sounds very hard at first,
but at the same time it is a great consolation, since leaving the gap unfilled preserves
the bond between us. It is nonsense to say
that God fills the gap: [God] does not fill it,
but keeps it empty so that our communion
with another may be kept alive, even at the
cost of pain.   — Dietrich Bonhoeffer[1]

Many years ago, in my first book, *Releasement:
Spirituality for Ministry,* I wrote a reflection on
pain. It was entitled: "Pain: On Letting It Be."
This last year or so, while I was letting go of my
dearest friend and then trying to get used to the
empty space of her absence — to the gap that,
as Dietrich Bonhoeffer assures us, God will not
fill so that our communion can be kept alive —
I returned to this essay hoping to live up to its

title. I was clearly much younger, both in spirit and in years, when I first reflected on pain and on the blessings that come when one can dwell in it rather than pressure oneself to avoid it. Years of growing have invited me to live into the meaning of this in unexpected ways.

Going into the Pain

Life has a way of stripping all of us of our assumed strength and capacity to handle pain. It teaches us powerlessness, littleness, surrender to what "must be" in spite of our resistance and our pleading. It invites us through the agony of all this, almost paradoxically, into the tenderness of God, into that softness of heart where God can be found. Perhaps that is why those who mourn, the sorrowful, are called "blessed," and why the gospel, in spite of the fact that it promises consolation, makes no pretensions about doing away with sorrow. Instead, it invites us into the experience.

It took me a long time and a good deal of living and struggling before I began to understand what it means to "go into the pain," into the eye of its storm, if you will. The bias that our culture as a whole has built up against pain and my own personal tendency to distract myself from it in order to circumvent it were difficult to over-

come. Slowly, very slowly, however, I began to
see that "going into the pain" does not mean that
we have to "wallow" in it. Nor does it imply that
we ought to spend our energies primarily in fig-
uring it out — "getting a handle on it," if you
will. If one deals with pain purely intellectually, I
learned, one represses its depth and its grace.

Perhaps the most difficult lesson about pain
was the discovery that it does not go away, nor
is it transformed, when we lash out at those we
see as responsible for it, those who inflicted it
on us, or even those who did nothing to prevent
it. Earlier in this book we reflected on the importance of forgiveness in the redemptive process
and on the false expectations that come with revenge that parades as justifiable punishment. We
know today that whatever energy exudes from
us *returns to us.* Anger begets anger and therefore increases. Revenge begets revenge. Hatred
fosters hatred. Violence only increases to more
violence and ultimately permeates the environment with negativity. It does not matter whether
the negativity comes from the person we see as
the criminal or from the society that punishes him
or her. "God is not mocked, for you reap whatever you sow," Paul tells the Galatians (Gal. 6:7).
Surrounding pain with negativity, therefore, only
increases negativity.

"Going into pain," on the other hand, points

us into depth. It means gently allowing the pain
to *be* there — the wound, the gap, the homesickness, the yearning, the deep loss — without guilt
or the need to control. It means walking around
in it, softly, and giving it permission to be felt,
welcoming its "tenderizing," its gentling presence
and the gift of tears that it brings. It means being
in the silence of one's inner being and encountering one's heart. It means finally seeing what
others have gone through, seeing it from inside
out, and connecting with our own long-neglected
empathy — that insight that comes with emo-
tional identification, the "aha" whispered in the
soul and pointing to solidarity.

We encounter a strange paradox when we go
into this experience: Pain hurts. We have always
known this, yet perhaps never with such agony
as when we embrace it. But pain, when accepted,
when gone into, is nevertheless a blessing. One
might say that pain simply *is:* that it is neither
good nor bad in itself, but simply is part of living life to the fullest and, as such, is a blessing.
I said earlier that suffering for the sake of suffering is waste, but that suffering for the sake of
Love's transformative power is divinizing. Pain
as an agent of growth, as a gentling and soften-
ing power stands in the service of Love. As such
it transforms. And so the gospel tells us that, in
order to become who we truly are meant to be,

we must "die," that we must be "baptized" in Christ's bath of pain (Mark 10:38).

Earlier we reflected on John 21:15–19, the passage where the resurrected Christ tells Peter by which death "he would glorify God." There is no shying away from suffering in this conversation, no sparing of pain. It is instead for all of us an invitation into the Christ story — a story that has Jesus himself become the "grain of wheat that must die." In the mystical sense of it all, one might say that he too had to feel utterly forsaken and alone, betrayed by his friends, abandoned by God *before* he could rise. And in the totality of this he became the symbol of the human journey: "To hell and back," is how my friend Clare used to speak of it. She was describing the agony of depth-living that ultimately, and only through freedom — always in the process of freeing itself — leads to authenticity, to the hard-earned transcendence that is maturation.

Does God Suffer?

Was Christ's suffering and, by extension, is our suffering necessary because of sin, I used to wonder when I was younger, or does suffering have something to do with holiness? Perhaps such a juxtaposition is artificial now. Considerations about the necessary connection between holiness and pain are, however, often allowed to lie fallow. This is largely because of the somehow unpleasant implication that God in some way approves of pain and also, I believe, because it could lead us to consider not only that God (in Jesus) suffered but also that God, in fact, experiences pain.

The traditional interpretation of pain sees it as a lack, an incompleteness. How, then, we ask, can God (the "Perfect" One) suffer? A further question that flows logically out of the same tradition and was answerable only by an association of pain with sin, is this: How can God allow those God loves to suffer? Unless pain is associated with sin, and sin attributed to humankind, God will appear to have willed it. Within the contemporary Western cult of pleasure which, strangely, seems to have permeated all thought including, I suspect, some of our theologies, this would be tantamount to accusing God of willing evil.

But why should pain be evil? Perhaps, as I have suggested above and as the scriptures seem to indicate, it is necessary and can, in fact, be good. This would allow perfection and pain to be reconciled, and one could then reflect on a "suffering God." Our own pain would also no longer have to appear negative — as punishment for our sins, the sins of others, or as unhappy by-product of an imperfect universe. Although these explanations may remain as possibilities for some, pain could also legitimately be encountered on a deeper level, namely, within holiness as such.

Jesus called "blessed" those who sorrow, while at the same time he busied himself in healing many of their afflictions, even raising some from the dead and restoring them to the sorrowing. He assumed the cross, yet he also prayed to be delivered "from this hour." Nevertheless, and paradoxically, he challenged others to take up their cross as he had done, to assume pain, to die, and thus to glorify God. Where can one find an explanation for these seeming contradictions? I have wondered of late whether perhaps logic escapes us here and speculations fail us because the matter is beyond logic and speculations. Is there perhaps a mysterious dynamic between the sorrow and the comforting — a pain entered in upon, held within oneself, acknowledged, embraced without fear — that makes for the blessedness?

Christ's repeated exhortation while among us was "fear not." Might he have come primarily to liberate us from the fear rather than from the pain and suffering toward which it is directed? If this is so, one would really have to distinguish between two dispositions toward pain and sorrow that are integrally related to holiness or its betrayal and, therefore, to the struggle for God's reign. One disposition would be marked by the flight from pain characterized so often by our denial or anger, by our projecting blame and responsibility for it onto others, by self-hate, the hatred of others, and the blaming as well as the rejection of God. All these seem essentially related to the fear and consequent avoidance of pain from which Christ came to free us. Fear debilitates. It has some run away and forsake the just cause. It has others attack (quite often the innocent) in order to protect themselves. It cannot be creative, therefore, for it lacks the energy that comes with courage and its ability to risk for the sake of love.

The other disposition would be found in an acceptance of pain. By this, of course, I do not mean a morose and unhealthy search for pain and suffering. Masochism is self-absorbed and lacks the autonomy necessary to take personal responsibility and pursue further growth. The acceptance of pain, on the other hand, penetrates, as it were, into its center. It holds itself there in quiet openness and freedom. Thus it comes to discover that it, in turn, is held and sustained by a strength which can only be ascribed to grace: "for they shall be comforted."

Pain and the Holy One

What then of the possibility that God not only is capable of suffering, but that, in fact, *pain is of*

God, and that a denial or refusal of pain is an aspect of our brokenness and fear, of our all too human humanness? Could it be that pain, indeed, is holy, not only in its consequences (God drawing good out of evil) but also in its purpose, and that the "perfection" of humanness resides in the embracing of holy pain, not for the sake of anything less than the breakthrough of God in us?

There seems little doubt that human beings whom we call "great" are great at least partially because of their encounter with pain. Psychologists tell us, and often personal experience does so as well, that the sensitive person — the one most "in touch" with his or her fundamental relationality — is also the one most in pain: What the dull ear cannot hear, the composer picks up in anguish or rejoicing; what the dull heart cannot feel, the lover endures with passion. Love, for that matter, is the example par excellence of ecstatic pain. The lover virtually stands outside himself or herself in a yearning for wholeness with the other. This, however, is brought about only, it seems, in the very acknowledgment of the pain. As Bonhoeffer points out in the citation above, the gap keeps our union with the other alive. When I say "yes" to my longing, the other is brought near, as it were, to my heart, for I acknowledge my need of her or him and recognize in anguish what I might otherwise have taken for granted. It seems that only the vulnerable can truly experience love, and that for those too self-assured, sufficient unto themselves, love often remains but a shell.

It continues to be a puzzle to me why we can so freely ascribe pain to the highly sensitive spirit, ecstatic passion to the lover, yet refuse it to God. Concerning this, the Russian philosopher Nicholas Berdyaev shares a superb reflection:

> It is extraordinary how limited is the human conception of God. We are afraid to ascribe to God inner conflict and tragedy character- istic of all life, the longing for the "other," for the birth of humankind, but have no hes- itation in ascribing to God anger, jealousy, vengeance and other affective states which, in us, are regarded as reprehensible.[2]

Berdyaev sees an amazing contradiction be- tween our view of personal holiness and our interpretation of the divine. God, we declare, is self-sufficient, immobile, almost tyrannical: demanding uncompromising submission. These attributes, however, we consider despicable when applied to humans. "People are afraid to ascribe movement to God, because movement indicates the lack of something, or the need for something that is not there," Berdyaev points out. "But it may equally well be said that immobility is an im- perfection, for it implies the lack of the dynamic quality of life."[3] Science today affirms the "dynamic quality" of a living universe. Why would or should its creator be any different?

Berdyaev sees "tragic conflict" in God as a sign of perfection. The God and Creator of life possesses the attributes of life holistically. God is dynamic, not immobile, flowing out in self-gift and yearning for all things to return to Him or Her. God, in fact, is revealed in our Christian tradition as "sacrificial love," which, "far from suggesting self-sufficiency, implies the need of passing into its 'other.'"[4] Sacrifice implies tragedy and tragedy implies pain. Sacrificial love, the birthing-pain of the creator, opens to fullness of life. It is Creator-pain. Nature — the handiwork of God — is, in fact, filled with pain. Its dying for the sake of life is a continuous rhythm, "cruel," no doubt, to thoughtless observers who, by projecting upon the flow of life their own inability or unwillingness to embrace creative pain, remain empty in their escape.

Sacrificial Love

A self-sufficient deity cannot create out of love, for love longs for union that self-sufficiency does not need. This is unthinkable to Nicholas Berdyaev, for it denies Christ the incarnation and all sacrificial love.[5] A union denied because

of freedom betrayed demands that Love assume
freedom in order to open the way of return.
Christ-love is sacrificial love, which embodies
the death-pain of this return. This is redemption: "Unless the grain of wheat falls to the earth
and dies it remains just a grain of wheat" (John
12:24).

Now if the dynamic holiness of God holds the
pain of tragedy within it, would it not follow that
God not only is capable of pain, but that pain also
is integrally of God as Creator and Savior? God,
as it were, flows out in longing for the free other
and, because this freedom has closed itself off,
God breaks through into finitude and into freedom: takes on its form, as it were, and becomes
the Way in pain and sacrificial love.

Human love is called to do likewise: to be
"baptized in the same bath of pain," to continue
the Good News and respond to the divine yearning by its own longing for its source. Human
pain is homesickness for its beginning in God. As
Richard McBrien says it: "There is no merely natural end of human existence. Human existence in
its natural condition [in its fundamental human-
ity] is radically oriented toward God."[6] Try what
we may, we will not rest until we rest in God.
The death we are called to endure, then, is the
death to separation and toward wholeness. The
human condition is the story of this "life-oriented

dying." It is the gospel individualized. It is the Christ-story in each of us.

Life, it seems, is a natural journey from ego building, from establishing oneself and gaining one's identity, to ego-transcendence — the discovery of one's depth dimension and the finding of one's self not so much in terms of action and success (doing), as in terms of being (finding one's vocation in who one is).* This journey is never an accomplished fact but an ongoing process of letting go, of dying toward deeper life and greater openness. Its pain is inherent in the creation process itself and is, I would maintain, the same pain as the one we have above ascribed to God.

Such pain is creative, for its yearning is to flow back into God who is its beginning and its end. As such, the recognition and acceptance of the limitations of one's achievements, of the ultimate powerlessness of the human condition, of the finitude of strength, influence, and control, even of one's most noble endeavors, is an anguish that opens the heart ultimately and utterly to return to its most ancient belonging and to the yearning for union with its Source that, in the agony of its longing, is already coming toward it.

Such pain is redemptive, for the acknowledg-

---

*Chapter 3 discusses these distinctions within the context of ministry.

ing of our limits opens us to freedom: a freedom deeper than the limitations and weakness we have experienced, a freedom that speaks of a holy abandon, of an obedience (a listening) to one's being, of a "letting go" born of repentance.

In acknowledging our limits we take up the cross of our own poverty; we become childlike; we let (in Jungian terminology) the ego surrender to the Self and, in Sebastian Moore's interpretation of this, we allow the crucifier in us to embrace the crucified in us.[7] Each of us says, in his or her own way, "I want to come home," and in stillness and in pain knows that his or her home is in the journey. Holiness as wholeness is a dynamic process. In sacrificial love we are holiness on the way.

Conclusion and Personal Application

What is it, then, that one should do about pain? Should one ignore the suffering in the world and simply abide in one's own recognition that ultimately pain is holy? The answer is hardly that simple!

To begin with, it is clear that suffering inflicted through injustice cannot be ignored. An unjust act is evil, and if it is within our power to put a halt to injustice, our integrity calls us to do this. This does not of course deny that pain endured by the oppressed can hold the holy within it, as was indeed the case with Christ crucified. But ours is hardly the role of judging what pain is or is not good for another. As far as our relationship with others is concerned, we are called to works of mercy even as Jesus was. We are not commanded to seek pain for ourselves either or to endure pain that could be alleviated. Masochism is an illness, not a virtue.

All this is not disputed by the considerations of this chapter. My concern here is simply with the pain inherent in life and in the life process. There is no doubt that life and vibrant holiness are pervaded with pain. Pain, as such, I am suggesting therefore, is of the holy and, if embraced, it sanctifies. It is my intuition that our own limitations (painful to us, without a doubt) carry within them the cut-off points for alleviating the pain of others. Our limits bind us, as they did Jesus. As the mystery of pain unfolds in our lives and in the lives of those we cherish, we often find ourselves suffering with the other whom we cannot help. Nowhere is this more excruciating than when a beloved — a child, a spouse, a friend — suffers and one cannot take away the agony, the dread, the discouragement, the sorrow. At such times, it may help if we can accept that pain is holy. Pain as holy is of the whole and makes whole, as Martin Heidegger would have us see:

Pain rends. It is the rift. But it does not tear apart into dispersive fragments. Pain indeed tears asunder, it separates, yet so that at the same time it draws everything to itself, gathers it to itself. Its rending as a separating that gathers, is at the same time that drawing which, like the pen drawing of a plan or sketch, draws and joins together what is held apart in separation. Pain is the joining agent in the rending that divides and gathers.[8]

In rending the heart, pain holds our love as one in the Holy. Through it we take part in the dynamic flow of life and learn compassion, the "perfection" of God. In our poverty we must trust that suffering leads the other, in ways we do not know, toward inwardness and wholeness. By surrendering ourselves to the pain of our incapacity to alleviate suffering we learn to let pain *be*. We say "yes" to its salvific, its creative dimension. Thus we release ourselves to the breakthrough of God in our lives.

Thoughts and Questions for Meditation

What are your thoughts concerning the following selections from chapter 6?

1. *Life has a way of stripping all of us of our assumed strength and capacity to handle pain. It teaches us powerlessness, littleness, surrender to what "must be" in spite of our resistance and our pleading. It invites us through the agony of all this, almost paradoxically, into the tenderness of God, into that softness of heart where God can be found. Perhaps that is why those who mourn, the sorrowful, are called "blessed," and why the gospel, in spite of the fact that it promises consolation, makes no pretensions about doing away with sorrow. Instead, it invites us into the experience.*

2. *Perhaps the most difficult lesson about pain was the discovery that it does not go away, nor is it transformed, when we lash out at those we see as responsible for it, those who inflicted it on us, or even those who did nothing to prevent it.*

3. *We know today that whatever energy exudes from us returns to us. Anger begets anger and therefore increases. Revenge begets revenge. Hatred fosters hatred. Violence only*

increases to more violence and ultimately permeates the environment with negativity. It does not matter whether the negativity comes from the person we see as the criminal or from the society that punishes him or her. "God is not mocked, for you reap whatever you sow," Paul tells the Galatians (Gal. 6:7). Surrounding pain with negativity, therefore, only increases negativity.

4. *"Going into pain," on the other hand, points us into depth. It means gently allowing the pain to be there — the wound, the gap, the homesickness, the yearning, the deep loss — without guilt or the need to control. It means walking around in it, softly, and giving it permission to be felt, welcoming its "tenderizing," its gentling presence and the gift of tears that it brings. It means being in the silence of one's inner being and encountering one's heart.*

5. *In the mystical sense of it all, one might say that Jesus too had to feel utterly forsaken and alone, betrayed by his friends, abandoned by God before he could rise. And in the totality of this he became the symbol of the human journey: "To hell and back," is how my friend Clare used to speak of it. She was describing the agony of depth-living that*

ultimately, and only through freedom — always in the process of freeing itself — leads to authenticity, to the hard-earned transcendence that is maturation.

6. *Jesus called "blessed" those who sorrow, while at the same time he busied himself in healing many of their afflictions, even raising some from the dead and restoring them to the sorrowing. He assumed the cross, yet he also prayed to be delivered "from this hour." Nevertheless, and paradoxically, he challenged others to take up their cross as he had done, to assume pain, to die, and thus to glorify God. Where can one find an explanation for these seeming contradictions? I have wondered of late whether perhaps logic escapes us here and speculations fail us because the matter is beyond logic and speculations. Is there perhaps a mysterious dynamic between the sorrow and the comforting — a pain entered in upon, held within oneself, acknowledged, embraced without fear — that makes for the blessedness?*

7. *Pain, as such, I am suggesting therefore, is of the holy and, if embraced, it sanctifies. It is my intuition that our own limitations (painful to us, without a doubt) carry within them the cut-off points for alleviating the*

*pain of others. Our limits bind us, as they
did Jesus. As the mystery of pain unfolds in
our lives and in the lives of those we cherish, we often find ourselves suffering with the
other whom we cannot help. Nowhere is this
more excruciating than when a beloved — a
child, a spouse, a friend — suffers and one
cannot take away the agony, the dread, the
discouragement, the sorrow.*

8. What is your reaction to the reflections at
   the end of this chapter concerning a suffering God, concerning Berdyaev's "tragic
   conflict in God," concerning sacrificial love,
   the birthing pain of the creator — pain as
   inherent in the creation process itself?

Notes

Preface

1. Karl Rahner, *The Practice of Faith* (New York: Crossroad, 1983), p. 63.

Chapter 1

1. Melvin Morse, M.D., with Paul Perry, *Transformed by the Light* (New York: Ballantine Books, 1992), p. 155.

2. Christian Wertenbaker, "The Eye of the Beholder: Paradoxes of the Visible Universe," *Parabola* 26, no. 2 (May 2001): 51.

3. Ibid., p. 52.

4. David Richo, *The Marriage of Heaven and Earth: A New Look at Christian Spirituality* (Kansas City, Mo.: Credence Cassettes), tape 3.

5. Najm Razi, 1256 C.E., quoted in Arthur Zajonc, *Catching the Light: The Entwined Story of Light and Mind* (New York: Bantam Books, 1993), p. ix, and cited in ibid., p. 44 (adapted for inclusive language).

6. A. I. Okumura, *Awakening to Prayer,* cited in "Friends of Silence" newsletter, 14, no. 1 (January 2001): 1.

7. Michael Himes, *Trinity*, videotape by Fisher Productions, Box 727, Jefferson Valley, NY 10535.

8. Barbara Fiand, *Releasement: Spirituality for Ministry* (New York: Crossroad, 1987), p. xi.

9. Barbara Fiand, *Embraced by Compassion: On Human Longing and Divine Response* (New York: Crossroad, 1993), p. 69.

10. Jane Marie Thibault, *A Deepening Love Affair: The Gift of God in Later Life* (Nashville: Upper Room Books, 1993), p. 180.

11. Barbara Fiand, *Wrestling with God: Religious Life in Search of Its Soul* (New York: Crossroad, 1996), p. 43.

12. Michael J. Himes and Kenneth R. Himes, *Fullness of Faith: The Public Significance of Theology* (New York: Paulist, 1993), pp. 82–83.

13. Reprinted with permission from the author. Translation from the German, B. Fiand and P. Hagenberger.

Chapter 2

1. Stephen Mitchell, ed., *The Enlightened Heart: An Anthology of Sacred Poetry* (New York: Harper & Row, 1989), pp. 38–39.

2. "Jesus atoned for our faults and made satisfaction for our sins to the Father" (*Catechism of the Catholic Church,* no. 615).

3. "Believing is an ecclesial act. The Church's faith precedes, engenders, supports, and nourishes our faith.... We believe all 'that which is contained in the word of God, written or handed down, and which the Church proposes for belief as divinely revealed' " (*Catechism of the Catholic Church,* nos. 181–82).

4. Gary Zukav, *The Dancing Wu Li Masters: An Overview of the New Physics* (New York: Bantam Books, 1980), p. 211.

5. Ibid., p. 186.

6. Diarmuid O'Murchu, *Quantum Theology* (New York: Crossroad, 1997), p. 127.

7. Louis de Broglie, *Einstein,* referenced here by Zukav, *The Dancing Wu Li Masters,* pp. 220–21: "In space-time everything which for each of us constitutes the past, the present, and the future is given in block.... Each observer, as his [her] time passes, discovers, so to speak, new slices of space-time which appear to him [her] as successive aspects

of the material world, though in reality the ensemble of events constituting space-time exist prior to his knowledge of them."

8. Danah Zohar, *The Quantum Self* (New York: Quill/William Morrow, 1990), p. 145, emphasis added.

9. Ibid., emphasis added.

10. Ibid., pp. 169–70, emphasis added.

11. Francis Thompson, cited by Arthur Zajonc, *Catching the Light: The Entwined History of Light and Mind* (New York: Oxford University Press, 1993), p. 319.

12. Zohar, *The Quantum Self*, p. 34.

13. Pierre Teilhard de Chardin as cited in Barbara Fiand, *Wrestling with God* (New York: Crossroad, 1996), p. 75.

14. Edwina Gateley told this story at the Northwest Catholic Women's Convocation in Seattle, April 28, 2001. Plenary Session: "Mothers, Midwives and Healers — Hearts on Fire: Women Journeying to Transformation and New Life."

15. William Johnston, cited in Barbara Fiand, *Prayer and the Quest for Healing* (New York: Crossroad, 1999), p. 125.

16. Rilke, as cited in Mitchell, *The Enlightened Heart*, p. 144.

Chapter 3

1. Sigrid Becker, "Evangelical Poverty" (my translation).

2. Thomas F. O'Meara, O.P., *Theology of Ministry* (New York: Paulist Press, 1999), p. 143.

3. Ibid.

4. Donald Nicholl, *Holiness* (New York: Seabury, 1981), p. 14, emphasis added.

5. Richard McBrien, *Catholicism*, vol. 1 (Minneapolis: Winston Press, 1980), p. 159.

6. Including yet also transcending his historical presence here on earth.

7. Martha Reeves, "Socrates and the Cheshire Cat or Abhorring Horror Vacui," William and Rita Bell Lecture, University of Tulsa Campus, February 29, 2000, p. 5.

8. Brian Swimme, *The Hidden Heart of the Cosmos: Humanity and the New Story* (Maryknoll, N.Y.: Orbis Books, 1996), p. 99.

9. Rupert Sheldrake, here cited by Willigis Jäger, *Search for the Meaning of Life* (Liguori, Mo.: Triumph Books, 1995), p. 26, emphasis added.

10. Jäger, *Search for the Meaning of Life*.

11. Teilhard de Chardin, as cited in ibid., p. 24, emphasis added.

12. Margaret Wheatley, *Leader's Guide: Leadership and the New Science*, video presentation, produced by CRM Films, Carlsbad, California.

13. William Johnston, *Silent Music: The Science of Meditation* (New York: Harper & Row, 1979), pp. 90–91, emphasis added.

14. Jäger, *Search for the Meaning of Life*, p. 27.

15. Ibid., p. 145.

16. Ibid., pp. 145–46.

17. Thich Nhat Hanh, *Touching Peace*, ninety-minute video presentation, produced by Legacy Media, Inc., Berkeley, California.

18. Hildegard of Bingen, cited by Diarmuid O'Murchu, *Reclaiming Spirituality* (New York: Crossroad, 1998), p. 85.

19. Johnston, *Silent Music*, pp. 132–33.

20. As cited in William Keepin, "Lifework of David Bohm: River of Truth," *Re-Vision: A Journal of Consciousness and Transformation* 16, no. 1 (Summer 1993): 34.

21. Michael Talbot, *The Holographic Universe* (New York: HarperPerennial, 1991), p. 14.

22. Keepin, "Lifework of David Bohm," p. 34.

23. Danah Zohar, *The Quantum Self* (New York: Quill/William Morrow, 1990), pp. 36–37.

Chapter 4

1. Petru Dumitriu, *To the Unknown God,* trans. James Kirkup (New York: Seabury, 1982), p. 242.

2. Martin Heidegger, *Holzwege* (Frankfurt am Main: Vittorio Klostermann, 1963), pp. 248–51, 294.

3. Armand M. Nigro, S.J., "That Hour with Jesus," reprinted with permission from the author.

4. *Catechism of the Catholic Church,* nos. 65, 66, 73.

5. Hindu Tale from Chandogya Upanishad retold by Rama Devagupta, "Nothingness," *Parabola* 25, no. 2 (Summer 2000): 59–61, retold with adaptations.

6. Brian Swimme, *The Hidden Heart of the Cosmos* (Maryknoll, N.Y.: Orbis Books, 1996), pp. 92–93.

7. Diarmuid O'Murchu, *Reclaiming Spirituality* (New York: Crossroad, 1998), p. 42.

8. Heidegger, *Holzwege,* p. 294.

9. Prince Louis de Broglie, "The Aspiration towards Spirit," cited in Ken Wilber, ed., *Quantum Questions: Mystical Writings of the World's Great Physicists* (Boston: Shambhala Publications, 1985), pp. 114–20.

10. Sir Arthur Eddington, "Defense of Mysticism," cited in Wilber, *Quantum Questions,* pp. 196–97.

11. Karl Rahner, *The Practice of Faith* (New York: Crossroad, 1983), pp. 78–79, emphasis added.

12. I am indebted in my discussion of metaphor in religious language to the thinking and very lucid explanations of Sandra Schneiders, *The Revelatory Text* (San Francisco: HarperCollins, 1991), pp. 29–33.

13. Ibid., p. 30.

14. Rahner, *The Practice of Faith,* p. 63.

15. Schneiders, *The Revelatory Text,* pp. 31–32.

16. Ibid., p. 35.

17. I refer the reader to an excellent treatment on the divinity of Jesus in the "Spirit Christology" of Roger Haight, *Jesus the Symbol of God* (Maryknoll, N.Y.: Orbis Books, 1999); of particular interest are pp. 458–65.

18. Schneiders, *The Revelatory Text,* p. 35.
19. Barbara Fiand, *Embraced by Compassion* (New York: Crossroad, 1993), p. 63.
20. Der Mond ist aufgegangen,
    die goldnen Sternlein prangen am Himmel hell
        und klar;
    der Wald steht schwarz und schweiget
    und aus den Wiesen steiget
    der weiße Nebel wunderbar.

    Wie ist die Welt so stille
    und in der Dämm'rung Hülle so traulich und so hold
    als eine stille Kammer,
    wo ihr des Tages Jammer
    verschlafen und vergessen sollt.

    Seht ihr den Mond dort stehen?
    Er ist nur halb zu sehen und ist doch rund und
        schön!
    So sind wohl manche Sachen,
    die wir getrost belachen,
    weil unsre Augen sie nicht sehn.
                                    — Matthias Claudius

Chapter 5

1. Arthur Zajonc, *Catching the Light: The Entwined History of Light and Mind* (New York: Oxford University Press, 1993), p. 5.
2. Ibid., emphasis added.
3. Sandra Schneiders, *The Revelatory Text* (San Francisco: HarperCollins, 1991), p. 32.
4. Jerome Kodell, *The Eucharist in the New Testament,* Zacchaeus Studies (Wilmington, Del.: Michael Glazier, 1988), p. 61.
5. Ibid., p. 63.
6. Elisabeth Schüssler Fiorenza, *Jesus: Miriam's Child, Sophia's Prophet* (New York: Continuum, 1994), p. 37.

7. Ibid., p. 49.

8. Elisabeth Schüssler Fiorenza, *In Memory of Her* (New York: Crossroad, 1984), p. 135.

9. Ibid., p. 136.

10. Ron Ashmore, "Viewpoint," *National Catholic Reporter*, May 18, 2001.

11. Julian of Norwich, quoted by Brendan Doyle, *Meditations with Julian of Norwich* (Santa Fe, N.Mex.: Bear & Company, 1983), pp. 76–77.

12. Ibid., pp. 82–83.

13. Brennan Manning, T.O.R., *A Stranger to Self-Hatred* (Denville, N.J.: Dimension Books, 1982), pp. 119–20.

14. Augustine quoted here by Garry Wills, *Papal Sin: Structures of Deceit* (New York: Doubleday, 2000), p. 141.

Chapter 6

1. Dietrich Bonhoeffer, *Letters and Papers from Prison* (London: SCM Press, Fontana Books, 1953), p. 61.

2. Nicholas Berdyaev, *The Destiny of Man* (New York: Harper Torchbooks, 1960), p. 28, adapted for inclusive language.

3. Ibid.

4. Ibid.

5. Ibid., pp. 28–29.

6. Richard P. McBrien, *Catholicism,* vol. 1 (Minneapolis: Winston Press, 1980), p. 161.

7. Sebastian Moore, *The Crucified Is No Stranger* (London: Darton, Longman & Todd, 1977), pp. ix–xii.

8. Martin Heidegger, *Poetry, Language, Thought,* trans. Albert Hofstadter (New York: Harper & Row, 1971), p. 204.